Sheila Hampshire is working in the arena of developing effective people, both within and outside organizations, through a process of coaching and counselling.

In her 10 years' personnel experience in industry, Sheila focused on the effective development of people and organizations. Her period at IPM in training and development activities enabled her to explore further these areas in relation to national, academic and business aspects. She then formed a consulting organization specializing in management development.

Sheila is also an Associate of the HRA Training and Development Group.

Tom Jaap has been involved with personal development activities over the past 25 years. He has specialized in developing methods to help people achieve the best from life by making better use of their potential.

Tom was trained initially as a design engineer, is a Fellow of the Institute of Mechanical Engineers, Companion of the British Institute of Management, and has a Master's Degree in Business Administration. He is also a visiting lecturer at Strathclyde University, author of books and articles, treasurer of the Scottish Community Education Centre, Executive Chairman of the International Federation of Training and Development Organizations, and regular contributor at international conferences and on radio and television.

Tom is Managing Director of the HRA Training and Development Group.

HOW TO REALIZE YOUR POTENTIAL

Sheila Hampshire
Tom Jaap

INSTITUTE OF PERSONNEL MANAGEMENT

First published 1981

Made and Printed in Great Britain by
The Anchor Press Ltd, Tiptree, Essex

Hampshire, Sheila
How to realize your potential.
1. Achievement motivation
I. Title II. Jaap, Tom
153.8 BF683
ISBN 0-85292-278-7

CONTENTS

LIST OF ACTION POINTS

ACKNOWLEDGEMENTS

The authors would like to acknowledge those who helped in the production of this book, particularly Mary Brooks and Linda Ford for the processing and typing of the manuscript.

Note

For the sake of convenience and style, the convention has been followed by using *he* and *him* to cover *she* and *her* wherever the context is appropriate.

INTRODUCTION

Realizing potential is about the future; it is about striving for dreams and ambitions of where we want to be and what we want to do, and of preparing our lives in such a way that we are motivated towards realizing our objectives and developing through the opportunities provided by change.

This book provides the means by which you can turn your dreams and ambitions into reality. One of the key aspects of this process is self responsibility. The authors consider that each person is responsible for the development of hidden potential from childhood throughout life. It is, therefore, a lifelong process and involves planning and achievement of your life overall as it affects various areas at different stages, at school, in college, at work, at home, in leisure, in the community, and in relationships. The book will help you to develop individual skills and those you require to relate effectively to others in a variety of situations.

The book will be of value to all who wish to realize their hidden potential and achieve fulfilment, whether they be young people at school or in college, people at work or out of work, or those in retirement. Each of us has our own unique development ladder.

Whatever step you are on at the moment, you have the capacity to achieve more from the rest of your life.

The development and growth of society depends upon the continuous development and growth of individuals. The capacity that human beings have to realize their potential means they can continue developing to cope with the rapid changes of life today and in the future.

You will become involved in the process of identifying your hidden potential by using the series of action points contained in the book. These are designed to help you focus on yourself, understand yourself better, and review the way by which your current life style will meet your future needs. The early action points concentrate on your current life position; the latter ones turn your attention to defining what you can achieve in the future and help you map the ways by which you can make it happen. This process can change the course of your life.

The deeper the thought you give to each action point, the more effective will be your learning and subsequent development. The process is continuous throughout your life. As you progress, you will increase your awareness because each event will help to clarify your real situation. The more you develop your self-awareness, the better equipped you will be to face the challenge of the future.

You are responsible for your life and can choose what happens in the future. 'Today is the first day of the rest of your life' and the rest of your life will happen whether or not you decide its course. Why not fill the rest of your life with the achievement of your hopes and ambitions?

1 RECOGNIZING POTENTIAL

Definition and identification of potential

Have you ever stopped to think about what is meant when the term 'has potential' is used in describing a person? It is a term applied to indicate that someone has done something special or shows the ability for achieving greater things. Most of us feel comfortable when saying 'he has potential' and know, in our own terms, what we mean. But is the meaning the same for others? Do they understand the criteria we have used in saying that a person has potential? The answer is most likely to be in the negative, for each of us perceives potential in a host of different ways.

The dictionary definition can help us to a clearer understanding. The word 'potential' is derived from the Latin **potens** 'power' and **posse** 'to be able to'. Potential means 'a force capable of coming into being or action, latent.' Further study of the dictionary gives 'to potentialize' as being to 'make potential, convert (energy) into potential condition'. We all have potential but as it is latent we cannot know its full extent and it needs something to convert it into action. Therefore we face the problem of these hidden factors in our own assessment when we describe someone as having potential. Our judgement will thus be subjective and the more subjective it is the greater the chance of it being inaccurate.

Objective methods have been developed which can measure intelligence, numeracy, literacy, manipulative skills, stamina and general physical strength. In fact, there are methods to determine how the human being performs in a whole spectrum of activities, whether at work or play. These measurements are valid for current performance but do not necessarily indicate the full achievement of which an individual is capable. We have evidence of the achievement of athletes over the years through the constant breaking of records; of scientists whose inventions break through frontiers, of the engineers who put man on the moon. This is part of the ample evidence showing that potential exists within every one of us.

Can we measure potential?

Potential cannot be studied in a completely scientific way or quantified in totally precise terms. However, by using a combination of subjective factors which are unique to each individual, coupled with more objective criteria, we can come close to assessing potential. Individuals' life styles will reveal how they are using their hidden resource and this can be measured against both types of criteria. The amount of progress measured will be influenced by how much of this hidden resource has been energized.

In the work environment, potential is continually assessed in terms of how a person could be advanced to assume greater responsibility. Measurement of potential is regularly based upon past results and paper qualifications. The academic world tends to judge potential in terms of the numbers of certificates the person has accumulated. Other factors used to assess potential are job performance, stamina, reliability, loyalty and ability to relate to others. Of course, there are many other factors involved in the assessment process but these will normally be specific to the position being reviewed. The central issue may still be related to past performance as an indicator of future potential. This means of assessment works if we are in a job or occupation which allows us the opportunity to express our abilities in an effective manner. If the situation is different and we are in a 'dead end' job, how can past performance really indicate potential? This is equally true in situations outside of work and employment where potential success is judged in terms of past experience. However, we should avoid the danger of being diverted by the perceived difficulty of being precise about measurement of potential. Our energy should rather be directed towards applying the necessary motivation to convert latent potential into achievement.

Why is potential a latent force?

Life tends to follow a similar pattern for most people, a pattern which inhibits the full use of potential. When born we have latent potential. The help, guidance, and support of our parents and friends enable the majority of us successfully to reach the stage of looking after ourselves. We are educated and trained for life by others who apply their skill and knowledge for our benefit. The factors which affect our development in the initial stages are very much dependent upon others. For the majority, this dependence is eventually replaced by growing and maturing into adulthood.

We all have the opportunity to develop and be successful to a greater or lesser degree. So, how is it that for the many who succeed there are many others who are less than successful? It would be interesting to explore each case in turn to determine the reasons given for failure. Many of these reasons will only be excuses which pass the blame for lack of achievement onto others. If we were to construct an experiment in which ten children were provided with an exactly similar upbringing, education and training, the outcome could not be predicted. The unknown factor would be the degree to which each individual applied determination and commitment to grasp available opportunities.

We can blame a whole set of circumstances for our inability to achieve. Many of these reasons could be evaluated to show that they did have an adverse effect on our development. There are many who are brought up in an environment which appears to make them disadvantaged. Yet there are examples of people from such backgrounds who have achieved more out of life than those from apparently more advantageous situations.

In the end, it really comes down to the individual and how he allows circumstances to affect his desire for achievement. We need to apply energy to release potential. If we plod along at a low level of activity, the mind and body will have few demands made upon them and will eventually become ineffective; when increased demands are made, they will have great difficulty in responding to these needs and could fail.

On the other hand, when we keep our mind and

body active, they are then more able to respond to the demand for extra. Our lives are very much regulated by the demands we place upon ourselves to achieve at work and play. The more we expect out of life and the more we put into it, the more the necessary resources seem to be available from our reservoir of latent potential. The key to its release is a belief in ourselves and our ability to succeed.

We all have potential

Have you surprised yourself by doing something which you believed you could not do? Have others ever surprised you by telling you how good you were at something? Have you ever been faced with difficulty and danger which called upon greater strength and courage than you believed you had? If you have experienced any or all of these situations, you have identified potential.

We all have the potential to achieve much more than we do at present and failure to do so stems from our lack of awareness. We perform our roles in different ways and often are unaware of the skill and knowledge we contribute. It takes others to identify this. It is not always easy to praise others for fine work or service and therefore many of us are totally unaware of the real impact of our performance.

The one occasion which clearly shows the potential within us is when we are faced with an emergency. An often quoted example comes from the USA where a young man was working on his large estate car. He needed to replace a tyre on a rear wheel. After jacking up the car and removing the wheel, he used his wife's car to travel to his local garage. His year-old son crawled round the large car and accidentally knocked the jack which slipped and caused the rear end to crash, pinning the youngster by the leg to the driveway. The wife heard the screams of the child and rushed out to see what had happened. Without thinking, she lifted the rear end of the car with one hand and removed the child with the other. Fortunately the child had not been seriously injured in the accident. The major talking point centred on how the mother could have lifted the estate car: afterwards, it took three men to lift the rear end of the vehicle to the same height required to release the child.

Although the above story was well documented and authenticated, there will be people who will find it difficult to believe. Yet the simple answer is in the fact that the woman did not think the task was impossible – she acted as required in the emergency. This is only one of many such incidents which have been recorded over the years. You may have experienced, observed, or heard of something similar and accept that people can draw upon a hidden reserve when an emergency arises. In an emergency, there is a clearly identified need for something extra, and in most instances we find the necessary ingredients to help us through. The same holds true whether the emergency is related to a crisis or to some positive situation calling for that little bit extra.

The main difficulty most of us experience is in making use of this potential in the everyday situation. We are provided with new opportunities which may require additional skills and knowledge, yet somehow we fail to draw upon our store of potential to provide what is needed. The obstacles we place in the way of tapping this are easily dislodged once we are aware of the tremendous reserves available to us and waiting to be released.

Belief in yourself

There is ample evidence to show that a strong belief in yourself and your abilities will enable you to 'move mountains'.

Self-belief is at the core of realizing your potential and providing you with the drive to convert latent talent into real action. There is a marked contrast between the person who is self-assured and confident of his capabilities and one who is the opposite. How many times have you said, 'I can't do that', or, 'It's too difficult for me', or, 'What will other people think?', when, in fact, the task was certainly within your capability. We are often too lazy or unsure of ourselves to attempt to do something which we could do really well.

If our attitude towards the task and our belief in ourselves is negative, it produces a swell of counter productive feelings and eventually frustrations which we cannot fully overcome.

Later in the book we will look at the process of developing an increasing awareness of your present abilities. This will include ways of helping you gain a much better understanding of your potential, and thus an increasing belief in yourself.

A positive mental attitude

Belief in yourself will be developed and strengthened by adopting a positive mental attitude. Our society is largely based upon negative reactions to situations where 'can't', 'won't', 'don't', 'impossible', 'no', and 'not worth trying' are predominant in our vocabulary. The academic terms through which our education system operates classifies many people both for themselves and for the outside world as less than able and thereby promotes negative rather than positive thinking. Teachers and parents are often more comfortable when being critical of progress and behaviour than when encouraging in positive ways.

In the world of work, it is often said that we never hear a word of praise, only criticism. When the boss calls for you to go and see him, the first reaction is to think 'What have I done wrong?' Many are conditioned to look for the worst in everything and everybody, yet all of us have probably been more successful in our own terms with our lives than we really know. Success is achieved in a whole spectrum of events and activities which relate to every aspect of life. We will explore the concept of success later and show how the achievement of any goal you set, in whatever area of life, is success. However, it is vital that you have extended your vision to include all possible goals and have a clear idea of what you want to achieve.

Knowing what you want out of life

You will develop a higher awareness of yourself based on the self analysis process suggested in later chapters. This awareness will rapidly increase as analysis clarifies and updates the data you receive about yourself. It is vitally important that you accept responsibility for seeking feedback on your performance in situations to enable you to build an accurate picture of yourself.

Knowing what you want out of life comes from developing an awareness of what you want to achieve. It is important that this awareness is developed in terms of all aspects of your life in order to build a composite picture. This picture will then form the basis of showing you where you are and will help you assess what goals you want to achieve. It is challenging to set your sights high and be adventurous.

Having worked out what you want from life in broad terms, you can then set about planning to achieve it. This does not mean that you are locked into one plan; you have the flexibility of adding new goals and adapting the plan as required. To achieve, you need a belief in yourself and commitment to your identified goals. We will explore the process for achievement later in the book.

This is your life

For your potential to be released and realized, a belief in yourself, a positive mental attitude and knowing where you want to go needs to be combined with your commitment to take responsibility for your life. Your life belongs to you and is under your control. You choose how your skills and knowledge are used to achieve certain results. Then you assess the effects this has on others in different situations.

The way you develop the component parts of your life is your decision. We have all experienced the excitement and frustration of choice and the feeling of being pulled in more than one direction. Accepting responsibility for your life and identifying its future pattern can initially result in some additional stress and you may feel threatened by this. The excitement felt through taking responsibility for your life will soon replace stress as you achieve fulfilment. However, this will remain a dream unless you take charge of yourself and shape your life to achieve whatever it is you want.

Planning to achieve

Having taken responsibility for your life you need to create the plan through which you will achieve your goals. Opportunities and realization of goals seldom happen overnight and therefore plans need to be based upon realistic time spans with defined stages leading to the achievement of each goal. Take as an example your desire to buy a new car which you would like delivered today. Unless you actively plan what needs to happen and how you are going to achieve this, it will not happen. For objectives to be achieved, you will need to plan. Patience and persistence will be useful ingredients to achieve your long term goals.

2 ITS APPLICATION TO LIFE

Does potential only relate to work?

Many people believe that potential is concerned only with the working scene. Yet this is only one main area of life. The other areas also involve us to an increasing extent and we have the opportunity of channelling our potential into these activities.

We are on the threshold of another revolution which will change our outlook on work. As new processes and techniques to lighten our working load are developed, we will soon discover that output can be increased and technological innovations can produce results which, in the majority of instances, require fewer people. Couple this fact with increasing world competition and it could be considered that some national production requirements would either be static or have low growth. The situation could be affected by a whole range of constraints or opportunities, but the certainty of sustained growth in trade is just not there. The present economic difficulties are being experienced by most developed countries. There has not, as yet been found a satisfactory national or international solution to the problem.

The overall economic situation is further complicated by the rapid industrial growth of many developing countries. They are able to produce goods of the highest quality and at a very competitive price. With an active and highly motivated labour force prepared initially to work for comparatively low earnings, they will have an economic advantage for some time to come.

The attention and effort of developed countries will therefore be focused on shifting from production to specialist technological development. This will lead to fewer traditional jobs and more of our time will be devoted to leisure or some other non-work activity.

The non-work arena

In many countries, there are ample opportunities to serve the community through voluntary work. We have a whole host of voluntary organizations in Britain, many of which are desperately short of help. So, this is an area of activity which could provide real fulfilment for many who are going to be unable to achieve fulfilment in traditional work. Voluntary work is not considered a leisure activity and that is why the term 'non-work' has been used to distinguish between them.

In developing a caring society, there will be increasing opportunity for us to become involved in non-work and leisure activities for the betterment of ourselves and others. If some of our latent potential were channelled into these activities we could witness a radical transformation in the quality of life. In the meantime we will all be faced with opportunities to use our skills and abilities in a whole range of new ways. Part of our success will be measured in satisfaction received in helping others.

The challenge of change

Many people feel trapped in the past and continue to evaluate present day trends against outdated criteria. However, we are involved in a dynamic new world and are experiencing the start of a relatively new revolution: the micro-chip revolution. The rate of development of new technology has increased to such an extent that we have extreme difficulty in keeping pace with it. In the past it often took from decades to centuries for an idea to be converted into practical results. Today the same process may take only a few years. Against this background it is not difficult to understand why many people have lost their way. They are trying to comprehend the present situation using a level of understanding and awareness related to the distant past.

The challenge which faces us all today is one which will affect all aspects of our life. No longer can we expect a lifetime of work to be available. Neither can we even hope for the same opportunities which our parents had. This is the core of the problem and at the same time presents exciting possibilities for the future.

The core of the problem

We are caught in the dynamic events of a world which is changing in frightening yet exciting ways. The practices of the past are no longer relevant to the present. We are therefore presented with an opportunity to shape society in a constructive way to meet the needs of the new future. This will require vision to think through the projected shape of the future against a present day level of awareness.

There will be great demands upon each of us to

change our attitudes to work and play. Many of us cling to the past experience where the balance was 25 per cent work and 75 per cent sleep and leisure time. The reality of today and tomorrow could mean a rapid and radical change where the proportions will be 13 per cent work and 87 per cent other activities. The balance of life for many is still measured against the past without taking account of today's realities. We need to see new technology as an opportunity to improve our quality of life rather than as a threat to it. There will be greater opportunities to develop our interests and hobbies and thus to recreate lively, caring communities. The focus of attention will shift to people's needs in the non-work areas as this transition occurs. This then is the challenge we all face and to which we must respond in a positive way. We will need to overcome the lethargy which a destructive and extremely negative society creates in people. Greed and jealousy breeds a disregard for others which stimulates a negative reaction from them. Indicators show that many people have become more and more concerned with themselves; they covet material possessions as a sign of success, become obsessed by the fact that some have more than they do and demand an unwarranted share. We should not let the failures of the past or the unpleasant aspects of society influence us adversely. There is also a great deal of evidence to show that society is developing caring facets. The challenge is one of unlocking ourselves from the shackles of negative thinking and behaviour, believing that we can change and start reshaping society to provide a worthwhile and fulfilling future.

The fact that a massive reservoir of potential lies waiting to be tapped should encourage you to face the future with confidence. Change is inevitable but by developing the necessary skills and knowledge coupled with a positive mental attitude you will be able to take opportunities for personal growth which will enable you to adapt and cope with the future.

Your potential and the future

Our objective in this chapter has been to confront you with the issues of today and the future which should challenge your thinking. To develop and grow in the future you will need to appreciate what is happening around you and to have a high level of self-awareness. You can identify the skills and knowledge you need and set out to acquire them. Your latent potential will be released as you start on the road to achievement and fulfilment. The next part of the book will help you obtain better self-awareness.

3 CHARTING YOUR PRESENT POSITION

Self analysis

To realize your potential requires a high awareness of what you are in reality. We often build a fantasy world on which to exist and use various façades to deal with people and situations. Development and growth requires confidence and therefore it needs to be soundly based on what you really are.

Therefore the first stage in realizing your potential requires self analysis and coming to terms with what you are now as a person and where you are in life. Look at the past and determine what you achieved and why, what you set out to do and have not done, which opportunities slipped through your grasp and what unfulfilled dreams and ambitions you still have.

Action point 1
Success and failure

Think about the successes, failures, opportunities and ambitions you have experienced or expect out of life. Consider each aspect against the whole range of activities of your life, home, work, school, leisure and community.

1 *Successes:* List your main achievements over the past 10 years and state the reasons for your success.
2 *Failures:* Identify the disappointments you have experienced over the same 10 years and list the reasons for failure.
3 *Opportunities:* List the opportunities which you feel you have missed, and give the reasons why.
4 *Ambitions:* Identify the unfulfilled ambitions you have and list them in order of importance to your future life. Add to each the reason why you want to achieve it.

A systematic review of the past will help you to realize where you are at present. The amount of information will depend upon your age and experiences. It is important to look at all aspects in order to see the trends and patterns which have become part of you and your life. How critical were they in shaping your life, how did you handle them and what were the repercussions?

Individuals should know themselves better than anyone else can. Yet the opposite is often true. The lack of a realistic self image of yourself will make you vulnerable because your plans will not have a firm foundation upon which to build. It is often difficult for people to accept where they are in life because they look too much at weaknesses and not enough at strengths. The important factor is to look at the reason why things happened as they did and to look for the learning points in every situation and build on them..

Strengths and weaknesses

We are all better at some things than others. An audit of your strengths and weaknesses in relation to skills, knowledge and experiences will help you to know how you perform when dealing with other people and in all situations.

It is important to check and obtain feedback on whether the way you perceive and analyse your strengths and weaknesses is a true picture. Too often we make assumptions about ourselves which are based on information we have not checked. We then assume that we know why people react to us in a certain way or why a situation has a particular outcome, when, in fact, the reasons are many and varied and may not even relate to us.

A way of acquiring feedback is to exchange information more freely with others on events with which you have been involved. We usually obtain feedback at work through our boss, colleagues and friends and it is equally important to obtain this information for other parts of your life to compile a complete picture.

Strengths and weaknesses will change during life as you develop as an individual and will depend upon the circumstances in which you are prepared to become involved. Analyse the past to look at how closely your strengths are linked to your successes and how these have been related to your overall needs and ambitions. Consider why some areas are weaker than others and review their influence on your life so far.

Action point 2
Strengths and weaknesses

Consider all the strengths and weaknesses which make you what you are today.

1 *Strengths:* List your strengths and give reasons why you think that they are strengths.

2 *Weaknesses:* List the weaknesses and identify why you think they are weaknesses.

It is important to look separately at each part of your life. Often a strength is being displayed in one area but is lacking in a similar situation in another part of your life. Try and ascertain why this should be so. This should help you to become aware of your likely behaviour in a given set of circumstances. Knowing why you behave as you do will help you to change or develop in this area.

When you have reviewed each area of your life to date and looked at the reasons for success and apparent failure, you will have information on which to build. The most important aspect is to ensure that the data is 'real' and not 'make believe' because you can only develop and build on a sound and realistic foundation.

Are you 'switched on'?

Your current level of motivation and enthusiasm will influence how quickly you can progress towards achieving your identified goals. At the moment, which parts of your life 'switch you on' and why? Which parts are you ignoring and why?

An individual's motivation is influenced by what he is, what he perceives he is and his surroundings. Analyse those current and past factors which influence your motivation and thereby your direction and achievement in life. What material, spiritual and emotional factors are important to you at this moment? Why are they so important? Would you wish to change them, and if so, how?

Action point 3
Driving forces

We are all driven by the need to satisfy certain wants from time to time. Consider the driving forces which you have used to achieve what you want and those which have held you back.

1 *Self-motivation:* List the factors which motivate you to achieve what you want most out of life.
2 *De-motivation:* Think about factors which hold you back from achieving. Make out a list and identify why each factor actually acts as a de-motivator.

Review regularly the lists of what motivates and de-motivates you in the different aspects of your life and consider the reasons. Each list will be unique: no one else has led your life and no one else will feel about it in the same way that you do.

Look at all aspects of your life for it is worthwhile reviewing why you are motivated in one area and not in another. The analysis of these forces may help to explain your current situation.

Your present level of motivation will determine how quickly you can decide and work towards achieving your future plans. How long your present stage of motivation has existed will also influence this. The longer you have been de-motivated, the harder it may be to make a determined effort to change if that is what you decide you want to do. Still, it can be done and we will look at this later.

Influencing factors

Most people are influenced positively and negatively by experiences relating to other people in many situations and thereby have formulated a set of fixed principles on which they operate their lives.

Action point 4
Life principles

Consider:

1 The principles that you have and use in different aspects of your life.
2 List the factors which have had and/or are having a positive influence on your life and which could be of use in the future.
3 What are the negative influences.

It is interesting to note how in fact the same influencing factor can be either positive or negative depending upon circumstances and our mood at the time. Others will attempt to influence you throughout your life but it is your choice how much you allow this to affect you. It can, however, be useful for you to know why they desire to make you move in a certain direction. This may help you to choose the path you want to follow, to develop your potential and determine how much you want others to help you.

You have formed your own values, attitudes, belief and opinions throughout your life's experiences. You may not like all of them and you may wish to change some in the future. But it is important to recognize why you feel the way you do now and why you hold certain attitudes. Again, your total life experience has contributed to the formation of these beliefs and you should examine how you acquired these particular opinions. Are they in fact your own attitudes/opinions? Are they your parents', hero's, friend's, boss's, or whose? Have you consciously formulated these and therefore feel committed to them or have you allowed them to become part of your life by default?

Think again on where you are now and what your

attitudes are in reality. Are any of your attitudes in conflict with each other and preventing achievement?

Action point 5
Influencing factors

Draw from your range of life's experiences what makes you act and react the way you do. Relate to at least two experiences from home, work, school, leisure and the community which made you happy or unhappy. List the values, beliefs, attitudes and behaviours you adopted in each situation and the reasons you held and used them.

You may have been surprised at the difficulty you experienced in identifying the factors which made you happy or unhappy. Many of us are unaware that our behaviour is influenced by the attitudes we hold on a whole range of subjects. These attitudes in turn are formed from the values and beliefs we have acquired over time. We are, in general, very predictable people for most of the time. However, at times we seem to react and behave in unusual ways. This behaviour tends to be associated with the triggering off of deep and often subconscious values or beliefs Once our value system is under attack we respond to defend it and this response is likely to be based upon an emotional rather than logical reaction.

Consider how your list of values is linked to your behaviour. When you are angry with someone, think about the real cause of the anger and trace it back to the value or belief being challenged. The more aware you are of why you react in a particular way to certain actions, statements and behaviour of others, the more aware you will be of what influences your attitudes and subsequent behaviour.

Conditioning factors

You have been conditioned by your past experiences to have certain expectations of similar circumstances in the future.

The conditioning process operates initially in the family and school environment and then through college, work and leisure activities. When reviewing your strengths and weaknesses and looking at factors influencing your life, review how many of the reasons for your successes or failures have been affected by conditioning. Your reactions may be reflex actions. Think about areas where you feel at present you give a conditioned response and those areas where you make a free, creative reply or decision.

Action point 6
Conditioning

> You are still concentrating on self analysis at this stage. Make out a list of all the factors which condition you to act in a less than effective way. These may be areas which started in childhood or have been acquired recently.

An example of conditioning by society is the class system. This was created and upheld by appropriate forces which satisfied the needs of those involved. People were expected to behave and react according to their class norms and could only move between the classes and achieve acceptance once they practised those characteristics associated with their new class.

Parents also play a significant part in conditioning our life roles as boys and girls. Even now very few boys' parents encourage them to cultivate interests which are perceived as female related. The same is true of girls' parents discouraging them from involvement in 'male' pursuits. This behaviour conditioning and life style role formation can have adverse effects. If society and parents concentrated on the real needs of today rather than yesterday, they would look at their roles as parents in a different light.

Today we see the breaking of past conditioning by a greater freedom in society. The roles adopted by men and women are being reversed with many positive and some negative results. Although some of society frowns upon change there is an increasing awareness that there are exciting opportunities for development once the mystique surrounding life style roles is cleared. When you can identify your conditioning and its effects, this will help you identify your route to development.

Barriers

Existing within each of us in varying degrees are barriers which we need to identify if we are to plan our future on a sound basis. Again these barriers have been formed by our past experiences and may have prevented us from achieving in the past. More important, they may continue to prevent us from achieving in the future. The significance of a barrier in blocking your path will depend upon its nature and the length of time it has existed.

As you analyse the effect which conditioning and influencing factors played in the past you will become aware of how the mind creates barriers to progress. The mind will be able to reach all the negative memories and experiences stored in the brain. These will be dredged out to act as de-motivators and hold you back from attempting new ventures.

Look at one example of how the mind can work. If you are in love with another person who has not clearly indicated their love for you, the chances are that you will feel insecure. Whenever the other person does not provide answers which satisfy you on what they have been doing or who they have been seeing, this can develop your jealous feelings. Yet in reality there could be no valid reason for you to dissipate your energy in this negative way. The power of the mind to energize you to depths of despair or heights of elation should be recognized.

It is vital for you to know why you react in different situations. There will always be a reason for the attitudes and behaviours used and you should trace these back to your values, beliefs and conditioning. The more able you are to separate the real from the imaginary barriers the quicker you will be able to influence your mind positively.

Action point 7
Barriers

> You identified how conditioning may have affected your achievement. Extend your analysis to identify further factors which act as barriers to your progress. Think about each aspect of life and see what holds you back or diverts you from your chosen path. Try to find a reason for each barrier and how it adversely affects you.

It is important to identify current barriers in the above areas, or any others, which will hinder you changing, coping and developing.

You are what you want to be

You are what you want to be. Your beliefs, attitudes and behaviour act out the role you want from life. All the excuses used to explain or complain about your present position tend to camouflage the fact that you are there because you want to be. The basic decisions were yours. Some of you may wish to challenge this statement and explain how other factors influenced adversely what you wanted to achieve. However, whatever the reasons, you are where you are and what you are and it is this awareness of your true self and situation which you must accept.

Action point 8
What and where you are

> Review your responses to the previous seven action points and draw from them the information which helps you to understand what and where you are. Prepare a statement which describes yourself in terms of the assets you have and how these have helped you be where you are today. Draw out those liabilities which have held you back and identify the reasons.

In carrying out this self analysis you will unfold the picture of where you are at present and why. You should consider this an audit or stock taking of your life to date from which you can effectively plan the future. Be careful not to hide any areas of real concern because you feel uncomfortable about them. Equally, analyse the reasons for your success in life; this will help you develop a better self image, which in turn will increase your feelings of self worth.

Self worth

Irrespective of how self esteem, self respect or self awareness are described, we all have an image of what we think we are. With most people this image of themselves will be reasonably acceptable. However, in developing and maintaining this acceptable self image, we sometimes act and react in particular ways which can be destructive to others.

1 We rationalize our shortcomings and blame others for problems and misunderstandings in our lives. We fail to recognize how our own attitudes and behaviour are creating the unsatisfactory situations. We should look at ourselves before placing the blame on others.
2 We snigger at, bully and oppress others who do not follow our way and meet our demands. We can place intolerable strains on relationships by attempting to make others conform to our wishes without due regard to their needs.
3 We attempt to bring others down to our level by persecution, criticism, nagging and gossip. Character assassinations are often based upon our own feelings of inadequacy, guilt, greed, jealousy or anger.

When we fail to force others to conform to our norms, our self image is threatened and we may take measures to run away from ourselves through drink, drugs, or any other form of escapism. In the final analysis there is no way we can develop a good self image on the basis of being destructive to ourselves or others.

You will develop and build your self worth by doing well and achieving effective results which receive deserved praise. If you identify yourself with positive goals, particularly if they are pursued with determined effort, you will eventually be successful. As each goal is accomplished and your relationships developed in a positive way, feedback will reinforce your motivation to achieve and continue to strengthen your self image. A feeling of worth can also come from the trust, understanding and support given by those with whom you work and associate.

Using your potential

Your awareness of yourself and your life will be high when you are aware of the total situation within which all aspects of your life interact. This awareness will provide you with a realistic base from which to look at the future from a more objective viewpoint and develop your plans accordingly. There is no single right answer.

Start to make decisions on how to lead your future life based on the above analysis process. You know now the answer to the following questions in terms of how happy they make you feel about the present. Have you achieved what you set out to do? Was that really what you wanted to do? How frustrated do you feel? How much are you blaming others and situations for lack of achievement?

The way you release and realize your potential is determined by you. You may want to concentrate on one part of your life more than others. Whatever you want for yourself is there to be achieved once you recognize that your potential can be realized. You should now have a better picture of your current situation and what is influencing it. You may also have a better idea of what it is that you wish to achieve in the future and how this will provide personal fulfilment.

As suggested before it is highly unlikely that you are now anywhere near the point of using your potential to the full. A later chapter discusses how to decide what you want from life. The analysis of where you are now should give an indication of what is and is not possible. You are free to choose the course of the rest of your life based on what you are and could become. Whether you decide to do something or nothing is your responsibility. The choice is yours, but you will find the value, excitement and benefits to be gained from a responsible life well worth the effort required to develop and grow.

4 LEARNING FROM LIFE'S EXPERIENCES

Life skills

As you begin to focus more sharply on where you are at present, you can extend your analysis into the skills used in everyday situations. We acquire a wide range of skills which enable us at least to survive each day of our lives. The person who achieves little and constantly feels insecure will be using skills to a lesser degree than does the more competent and successful person. Therefore the range and degree of proficiency in the use of skills will be reflected by our degree of effectiveness.

We all have the opportunity to acquire skills which will equip us to meet life's challenges with confidence. Many of the skills are already within us as a part of our natural self. However our conscious self can restrict the use and development of these natural skills, holding us back from a higher level of achievement. The greater our self awareness becomes, the less we shall be working in the dark. The more we explore the past in a constructive way, the more we will understand what makes us tick. To help increase awareness and extend skills, this life skills arena will now be explored.

Range of skills

Few people are really aware of the extensive range of skills which they are constantly acquiring and using throughout their lives. Many of these skills were acquired during early childhood and have been developing ever since.

As you progress through life and become actively involved in various activities, you adapt by extending your range of skills. The more effectively you use those skills the more likely you will be to achieve the desired results. The skills are acquired in various ways; some come naturally and require very little effort to maintain at a high level of effectiveness; others have to be learned and reinforced continually to ensure a satisfactory standard.

Action point 9
Life skills

> List the skills which you feel you have now. These can be of any kind of physical or mental skill. Make your list as extensive as possible; the greater number of skills you identify now, the better equipped you will be to plan for the future.

There are also certain specific times which significantly influence the standard and range of skills you acquire as you progress form birth to maturity. The skills you have today reflect how the people involved at each stage expressed their concern for your development.

Home

Home is the place where the foundation for your future development was laid. Love and affection influenced your development in a positive way and secured for you a sound foundation. Conversely, without such a basis your development could have been severely affected.

Consider the range of factors which have influenced your development as a person.

Action point 10
At home

Describe how each factor listed below affected your skills. Identify the level of influence and how this was applied by those involved. You assessed earlier what your values and beliefs were. This action point and the others in this chapter will provide you with a further opportunity of reviewing how incidents and people help form your value systems. Go back to earlier action points and amend what you wrote to make it more meaningful. You may want to ask those involved to give you their reasons for attempting to influence your development: this will provide further feedback and enable you to check the facts or assumptions.

relationship with parents
relationship with brother/s, sister/s
relationship with relatives
relationship with friends
influence of each parent
your attitude to your parents
type of upbringing
discipline at home
was home a 'home'?
attitude of elders to you
social status enjoyed by household
financial security
availability of holidays
availability of travel at home/overseas
time allocated to activities at home

You can extend the list by as many factors as you

consider necessary to increase your awareness of what influenced your development. Some factors will be very significant in terms of their positive or negative influence. It can be very useful to identify these because they will help you trace the reasons why you are what you are.

After the early formative years, you will then be exposed to the second, and equally significant area of influence on your development: education.

Education

You may have many pleasant memories of your education and of your achievements, or you may have chosen to draw a veil over the whole period. Whichever is true for you, it will still be beneficial to assess the factors which created these feelings and attitudes.

Action point 11
During education

Education can play a significant part and sometimes a less than productive role in your development. However it is valuable to assess just how effective school, college or university were in developing you. Consider the following list of factors and identify how and when each one affected your growth as a person. Seek out the parts which helped you to develop skills and relate these back to Action point 9 for addition or amendment.

type of school and its objectives
educational system
single sex or mixed school
full-time boarding or day attendance
standard of teaching
attitudes of teachers to you

attitude of fellow-pupils to you
standard of discipline applied by staff and pupils
competitiveness of system
your academic performance
availability of sport and leisure facilities
your social involvement
your involvement in sport
were you encouraged to study arts, crafts and music?
opportunities for leadership
opportunities for developing self, for example, debating, chess, drama activities.
add to above for college or university

The points you have recalled provide a picture of the people and events which influenced your development. There will be some areas which had a greater impact than others. Identifying these will help you to know why you act and react the way you do. If you can then compare with a school or college friend, this will help to clarify further your understanding of what took place during those years.

These factors will have influenced your route through the education system and your choice of occupation.

Work

For many people, work consumes a significant part of their time. Its influence is considerable and affects how they lead their lives. You will find out how it has influenced you through completing the next exercise.

Action point 12
At work

If you are employed or provide a volunteer service

you are contributing from your store of skills and knowledge. The part that work of any nature plays in your development can be very significant indeed.

Consider each factor listed below and describe the reasons why you followed a particular course of action, or how a particular person affected your development.

first job
type of career followed
training received
further educational involvement
number of jobs held
length of time in each job
your attitude to the work
your attitude to supervisors
your attitude to subordinates
your attitude to peers
work environment
nature of the work
promotion prospects
development potential
public/private sector
attitude to unions
involvement in a union
time you allocate to work

This analysis will help you define in clear terms the influence work has had in shaping you as a person. Identify clearly the turning points in your career and consider their impact upon your progress. Then assess the influence of others. By doing this it will become apparent how you have built your current skill level relating to your job and in dealing with people, how you have allowed work to shape your life and how you have developed your life to cope with work.

Leisure

The time you allocate to work will naturally influence the time you have for other activities outside the work environment. This will, in turn, show the influence or otherwise which leisure activities have played in your development.

The following study should help you build a picture of your skills acquired at leisure and how these are integrated into other aspects of your life.

Action point 13
At leisure

Assess how you have been influenced by the factors listed below. Think about how each factor impacts upon the other factors and try to understand the reasons why your interests have developed in certain ways.

number of close friends
your attitude to friends
their attitude to you
number of acquaintances
range of leisure activities you have attempted
level of skill you have acquired in each
range of leisure activities available to you
range of leisure activities pursued by you
part played by parents and relations
involvement in voluntary organizations
involvement in church and its organizations
your attitude to sport
your attitude to music and dancing
individual activities followed
how much time do you spend watching/listening to TV/radio?
general use of leisure time

Extract from your analysis your attitude to, and skills used in, the range of leisure activities you pursue.

This will indicate whether you favour team or individual activities and whether you are competitive or participative.

Community

Involvement in the community is another major area which will influence your development. A few people opt out of society and become recluses, but the majority of us, to a greater or lesser degree, play some part in the life and activity of the community in which we reside.

Action point 14
In the community

Once again there are many factors drawn from your community experiences which have a part in your development. Consider the questions below and use your responses to chart important events which may have contributed to, or restricted, your growth.

urban or rural community?
type of community identity?
is it a welcoming community?
is there a strong influence through organized activities?
do you identify with the community, and why?
are there jobs, education and leisure opportunities available?
how long have you stayed in the one environment?
how many times have you moved to different areas?
how many different community environments have you experienced?
was it a sharing community?
were you involved in community activities?
how involved are you now?
what leadership do you contribute?

how much time do you allocate to community activities?

This analysis will enable you to have a clearer idea of how much of your time you spend on community activities and of your feelings on this aspect of your life.

Why you are where you are

You should have a greater awareness of why you are where you are.

Action point 15
Why you are where you are

Draw together details of who and what influenced you most during each stage of your life. This can be done by building a picture of each phase of your life, say every five years, from the five listed areas (home, education, work, leisure, community) Review the significant turning points in your life and relate these to the people who were involved. This process will identify the people who have played and may still be playing a positive part in your development. You will also perceive some people who may actually be, have been or are being, less than helpful.

This analysis will be useful to you when considering your future course of action.

How skill and knowledge are acquired

There is a dynamic element to the acquisition of skills from the various areas identified in this chapter. None of these areas can be static as people and situations are ever-changing. It should also be recognized that others play a significant and crucial part in the development of your skills, especially during the early part of your life.

As you grow you will try to do different things you observe others doing. All of us learn this way and it is the process of experiential learning which comes from observing, doing and then learning, through the techniques of translating knowledge into action.

We gain knowledge from a wide range of sources: newspapers, books, teachers, parents, friends, TV, radio and cinema. Some of this is gained in a disciplined way through structured learning at school, college or university. Other disciplined learning can be obtained through parental efforts or organized activities. The retention of information is influenced by the level of motivation. When faced with important examinations, the results of which could affect your future, the motivation is high and therefore the likelihood of retention is greater. However, after completing the examination successfully, the incentive has disappeared and the knowledge could be submerged in the dark corners of the mind never to be dredged up again.

The retention of knowledge is also linked to the level of understanding about the subject. The greater your interest and desire to know about something the more likely you will be motivated to understand and retain the information. How many times have you been surprised by the depth of knowledge a friend has disclosed about some hobby? The absorption and retention of information and understanding about a subject is in direct proportion to the level of interest.

Skill acquisition can be achieved much more effectively when you have an interest in the skill and a desire to achieve. The greater your level of motivation the higher the chance that you will acquire the skill successfully. For example, you will not be content just to demonstrate the skill but will practice it and seek out information and help which will enable you to become more proficient.

A belief in yourself, willingness and determination coupled with self responsibility will enable you to master most skills to a level appropriate to your physical and mental capacity.

Setting life goals

In the first chapter we learnt that potential is latent within us all and its release is dependent upon our awareness of what we can achieve. Your development as an individual can take many forms and be in one or more of the areas described in this chapter. Development in one sphere of life can have considerable benefits for your achievements in other areas.

Action point 16
Expectations

1 Prepare a list of what you now expect out of life – home, work, leisure, education and community.
2 Whenever you get another idea of what you would like to achieve, add it to the list.

This list will be used in a later part of the book to help you realize your potential.

As well as being aware of what we can achieve, we need to recognize the fundamental issue of how it will be achieved.

When you set out to achieve your targets, you will need to prepare a plan of campaign to help you accomplish them. You will become more aware of the need to set lifelong goals which enable you to give and receive much more from life. Thinking in terms of total life will provide you with a deeper understanding of life, of yourself and of how others fit into the picture.

Ownership of our development

Be prepared to recognize and accept responsibility for your own development. Otherwise, there is a danger that you will abdicate the responsibility to others. The end result will be unsatisfactory because you will blame others for your apparent failures. In most cases you will need the help of others to achieve your objectives, but be aware that in the process, you must retain full responsibility for your progress.

During the process of development be constantly aware of the pressures which can be exerted on you by your family and friends to abdicate responsibility and place some of it on them. 'Ownership' is often used to describe a possession or an object. The term can be equally applied to the goals set by an individual referring to their acceptance of personal responsibility for their accomplishment. Others may naturally want a share of the ownership because your success will reflect upon them to a greater or lesser degree.

Parents are the most likely to demand in overt or covert ways ownership of their children's achievements because it reflects upon their contribution as parents. This is normally based upon the parents' desire to protect and develop their children. The negative element only appears when their natural instincts begin to hinder the development of the child by restricting the options available. Parents must be sensitive to the needs of their children to ensure that they are given the freedom to fail so that they can learn how to succeed.

We all need help from others to achieve our goals, but this help must be provided without claim of ownership. It should be freely given without a reward being expected. In the natural turn of events, those who help are often themselves helped as the following story illustrates:

The empty hand

A group of salesmen met once a month for the purpose of discussing sales problems, types of sales resistance encountered and methods of overcoming them, new products or side lines appearing on the market and new phases of sales psychology. Many of the men were in similar or competitive lines of business, so they were careful to see that the helpful information they offered was of a general nature. For example, no mention was ever made of a specific individual or company as being in the market for a certain type of equipment.

One evening a member arrived with a guest, a man whose outstanding sales record in a highly competitive field was recognized by almost every man present. The guest's opinions were asked on almost every debatable subject.

After the meeting two men employed by companies competing with his own stopped to shake his hand and congratulate him on his remarkable success. He chatted with them for a few minutes and, to their amazement, told them about a company opening a new branch which would be in need of their product.

Later his host, who had listened to the conversation asked him why he had given his competitors such valuable information. 'Those fellows will be down there tomorrow morning, trying to sell to that new company', he warned. 'It may mean you'll lose a sale'.

The guest smiled at his host's blank look. 'They're both young, working their way up the ladder I've already climbed', he pointed out. 'They need a little boost now and then. Early in my selling career I found I never lost anything by helping the other fellow. As a matter of fact, I've kept a diary now for ten years. I can prove that for every tip I've passed along I've made two good sales myself, I've yet to see a helping hand remain empty.'*

When help is given in such a free and genuine way it can help you grow. You gain a great deal from people who are prepared to give something of themselves without looking for rewards.

The skills arena

How you use your time can point to how you think about your development. If you are keen, you will maintain a healthy and active body and mind, and this, in turn, will help you to assess opportunities for continued development in each sphere of life. Your self-awareness will be increasing as you examine yourself against the areas considered in the chapter and you will realize that many opportunities for self development are available. The more you understand yourself, the better you can understand how you react and relate to others. You are now aware of the range of skills which you have developed to some degree. However, there are many more which are

* LADANYE, Thomas W, ed. *Plain Talk.* Thomas W Ladanye, 1980.

under-developed or even undiscovered. The more you can develop your skills, the more effective you will become in dealing with life and in achieving results. The next three chapters explore in detail skills relating to yourself, relationships and situations.

5 INDIVIDUAL SKILLS

Focus on you

To begin any form of serious self-development you need a clear understanding of what you really want to accomplish. The chances of success are in direct proportion to the clarity of your goals coupled with your level of motivation to achieve them. The sharper you visualize your journey's end, the better you can define your route to get there and what you need to acquire on the way.

You need to be able to translate clearly the present into the future and this will require an injection of creativity and enthusiasm. The need for vision is vital because you will become what you see yourself in the future. Many will find no difficulty in visualizing what they want to become because they have an active imagination. Others will face considerable frustration because they just cannot build pictures of the future. Whatever point you are at, you can learn to develop the skills to visualize what it is you most genuinely want to achieve.

Vision development is closely linked to a base of self-understanding. The better you know and understand yourself, the better will be your ability to construct pictures for the future. The process of understanding and developing yourself begins with you. You possess a whole range of individual skills which you use to live your present life. How effectively you use and develop your skills depends upon your ability to know yourself.

Action point 17
Skill summary

Look again at the picture of who you are and what skills you have by reviewing the work you did on all the previous action points.

Decide how you want the picture you have drawn of yourself to develop and change in the future. Reading this book will not change you but it does provide useful ideas to act as a catalyst to enable you to change yourself — but this will only happen if you decide to start the process yourself; only you can fully release your potential.

Why should you change?

The word 'change' is greeted either with wild joy and enthusiasm or deep gloom and despondency. We can be unsure what is expected of us when confronted with a development opportunity which requires change, or may even fear that by accepting the challenge we will emerge as different people. It is the unknown quantity of change which causes uncertainty and fear. By managing the change effectively, these anxieties can be reduced.

For example, attending a training programme may provide an opportunity to learn some new skills, techniques, and knowledge. If the programme is associated with behavioural subjects, you could assume that in the training process you will change and emerge as a different person. In some cases, you could decide to adopt your new style instantly and will be excited at the prospect of using these skills at home, education, leisure or at work.

Given that you did behave in a different way when you returned to work or home, what could this achieve? In the first instance, it could cause some uncertainty because you were 'different'. The level of uncertainty will depend upon the benefits offered to others by your new style. If it makes people more comfortable it could produce considerable benefits. On the other hand, if you are so different that the change is threatening to others, there will be very few benefits — probably only disadvantages. Change is a very personal thing and will achieve effective results only if it offers the benefit of stable and acceptable relationships with others.

Not much would be gained from an instant conversion which changed your personality to such an extent that it made others uncomfortable with you. If you do decide to change, it should be a carefully prepared process based upon a clear understanding of the end result. For change to be effective, you need to take account of people's changing reactions to you as you progress towards achieving your objective.

Action point 18
Changes for future needs

Refer back to Action points 16 and 17. What changes will you need to make to your life style, behaviour, skills and knowledge to achieve what you want out of life? List the changes and how they will affect you and others.

How to understand yourself

In chapter 3 you were invited to start the process of learning more about yourself by attempting to complete a number of projects. These were designed to help you compare what you dreamed about with what you had actually achieved. From these exercises, you could identify the reasons for your success or failure. It may take several attempts at answering the questions before you can develop an honest picture of the gap between what you hoped for and what you actually achieved. We all have difficulty in being honest with ourselves and we are influenced in our self-assessments by what we believe has been achieved. This is often a distortion of the real picture.

It is vital that we are honest with ourselves. We may believe that we can fool others but usually we can do so only for a short time. However, we can go on fooling ourselves and distorting the true picture for longer. We frequently believe that the picture we have created is what we really are whereas it is a façade not based on a real understanding of ourselves. The power of understanding yourself in a positive way is available if you take time and effort to discover the real you. This process of discovery can be painful as you peel away the layers of disguise which have been built over the years.

Action point 19
Understanding yourself

1 Spend a few minutes reflecting upon the last six people you met. Write down a response to the following questions and relate them to each of the six people. How did you approach each person? What did you expect to achieve from the meeting?

Did you let the other person know what your true objectives were? How interested were you in the other person's needs? Did you hear what the other person was saying, both verbally and non-verbally? How prepared were you to help the other person achieve understanding from the meeting?

2 Review your answers and assess whether in each exchange you were being your real self or presenting a façade.
3 How honest were the others being?

To know your real self in an effective way results in the development of great inner strength and confidence. This, in turn, will be apparent in the way you deal with others who will, generally, react positively to your growth. Positive reaction and feedback from others will help you to reinforce such effective behaviours, and so adapt and change the less effective patterns. Being honest with yourself is the first vital ingredient in the process of developing self-awareness.

Seeking feedback

Feedback from others will help you learn about yourself; the more you actively seek information from others, the more accurate will be your self-understanding. You are looking for honest and full comments on how the other person sees your life. So to achieve the best possible benefits from the feedback session, you should prepare yourself beforehand. Start by thinking how you would react if you were asked to give feedback. Assess your possible feelings and reactions to the request. This will give you an understanding of the restraints which you would place on the content and method of your feedback. Then think about the reasons and reassurances you would need from the other person to help you feel free to be honest in your feedback. Think of when and where would be the best time and place for the session and how to arrange this. Consider whether it would be better to give written responses for the person to study prior to the meeting. The aim is to make the feedback session as useful and honest as possible and there may be other specific factors you need to take into account.

Be prepared for the possibility of adverse feedback and that the information you receive may not match your perception of yourself. You will need to select a person who will be both honest and sensitive in giving the feedback. You should also include in the planning your possible reactions and responses to any unexpected feedback.

Action point 20
Seeking feedback

Review and amend the projects you completed in chapter 3. Think of a friend or a member of the family with whom you feel comfortable and who you think knows you. Explain why you are asking the person to comment on your life and attempt to set ground rules which enable the person to be honest with you. Plan this session to enable the exchange to be meaningful.

Action point 21
Clarifying feedback

1 Do a similar exercise with another person you trust.
2 Compare the two sets of findings. Where they coincide you can build a clearer picture of yourself based upon the feedback. Where the information conflicts you will need to find opportunities to check this in greater detail.

Asking others to describe how they see you will help you check the accuracy of your initial perceptions. However, remember that each person is a unique individual and will see you in his or her own way. However, you will soon discover that the reason why some people see you differently from others is affected by the way you relate to them. Think about the way you act and react with someone for whom you have very affectionate feelings. Compare this with how you would react if you felt hostility towards the other person. As we are unique individuals we will act and react to each individual in different ways. Sometimes the differences are very slight and would not be noticeable. In other situations the difference would be considerable and would be obvious to observers. By receiving feedback and comparing this with how you felt, a clear picture will emerge of how you appear to others. You will also learn to identify the reasons which cause you to react in the way you do.

Feedback from others is one of the most effective methods of finding out about yourself. However you must learn to receive feedback and process it to determine how it relates to the pictures being built. It is worth noting that you will also receive considerable feedback of a casual nature from others with whom you come into contact. This means of receiving feedback can often prove to be the most accurate, as those involved often give spontaneous responses. As your skill of processing feedback improves and you learn to differentiate the biased from the honest, the level of awareness of who and what you are will constantly improve. With patience and persistence in your search for feedback, learning about yourself will become exciting and meaningful.

Learning how to learn

As there is plenty of material dealing with the subject of learning from a theoretical and scientific angle our intention is to help you understand how you learn in practical terms.

Each of us receives information on a whole range of subjects which relate to everyday life. This information is recorded in the brain which stores and classifies it. When we do something which relates to our existing knowledge, we can draw the relevant information from the brain. However, if the information was not understood when it was received or its relevance only became clear later, retrieval may be more difficult.

At each specific moment we feed a great deal of information into the brain which relates directly to what we are doing at that time. Other information is also being received which may bear no direct relationship to the main activity.

The closer the information is related to experience, the more likely it is to be received, understood and successfully filed in the brain. There is much evidence to support the view that experiential learning is the most effective way of reinforcing the application of knowledge.

You can apply this to the theory of the process of self-awareness discussed earlier. Having responded to the questions about yourself, you sought feedback from others and compared the results noting similarities and differences. Then you took some items and expanded them and sought further feedback which increased your self-awareness. By thinking about yourself and actively testing and checking your conclusions with others, you were engaged in the process of experiential learning.

The same process applies to all the skill we acquire during our lifetime. There are very few people who have the natural talent to acquire skills other than through this process of learning by experience.

Learning is a very simple and natural process, but one which is tampered with as we grow. For the very young many activities are only learned by imitation of others. As we grow older, we learn to walk and talk. Just think about walking for a moment; how could we communicate the complex movements involved in words? It is almost impossible to develop a simple description which covers the multi-dimensional activity of walking, yet most young people master it in a very natural way. This may involve many falls but, in the end, these experiences help the person adjust the skills used to enable walking to be achieved safely.

How do children learn to talk? They do not understand the meaning of the words they use at first, yet they use words and eventually master a very complex language before being taught the structure at school. The main reason young people learn effectively is usually associated with the fact that they have an expectation that they can learn and their minds are not cluttered with irrelevant data.

Action point 22
Learning how to learn

1 Apply the principle of learning to the basic skills of literacy, numeracy and oracy by reviewing how you learned each skill and which you mastered best.
2 List the subjects and activities which you enjoy the most. Describe how you learnt about them and state the amount of time you allocated to each. Think about the time now required to main-

tain a satisfactory level of knowledge and skill.

3 Make an alternative list of subjects and activities which you dislike but were forced to learn about. Compare the time you spend on these and the level of skill acquired.
4 How does all this help you to learn more effectively?

Your best subjects were probably the ones in which you had a great deal of interest. You will have had enjoyment from the experience of learning these subjects or, alternatively, had some other motivation driving you to acquire the appropriate skills and knowledge.

However, as we grow older we tend to programme our minds with a mass of negative instructions based upon past experience. This then affects how we approach the learning of new skills. Let us consider how you approach a new sport. Someone may have encouraged you to try a game of tennis. You respond and eventually find yourself on a tennis court feeling very self-conscious. However, you find that eventually you can hit the ball over the net. Your interest increases to the point where you begin to enjoy the game and want to improve. Now there are a number of options open, from continuing to play with friends to taking lessons from a professional. Whichever course of action you take, the chances are that you will improve to a point beyond which you cannot go. This point may be well within your level of skill expectation and thus leave you contented with the result. Alternatively, you could be dissatisfied with your game and continue to strive to improve. A great deal of time could then be spent in practising the poor parts of your game while neglecting the good parts.

This emphasis upon practising to improve the poor elements of your technique, in whatever sport, is painful. If you were to allow other feelings to be in control, you would practice the good shots to make them better. As your game improves, you gain confidence and this then begins to affect positively those areas of the game which are less than effective. Once again, take some time to observe a child learn to play a sport and see how quickly he adapts to the game. Children have an ability to learn from observing and then repeating the stroke in a satisfactory way.

If you were able to approach each event with an open mind and use the time to visualize what could be learned, the chances are that you could develop a whole range of skills in an effective and speedy manner. Let the process of your mind and body help you learn and try to be less critical of how you do it. The critical part of your brain projects failure before you have the chance to show success. There are ample physical handicaps applied to most sports without adding further mental ones. You have the capacity to learn much more than you give yourself credit for. The opportunities for learning are impressive now and will increase in the future as society changes. By attempting each activity with a desire to learn and by developing your self-awareness, your capacity to learn will increase. Now is the time to re-learn how to learn and take the opportunity to grow.

Seek and you will find

As you become accomplished in learning more about yourself, you will become better able to seek, understand, and effectively use the knowledge you collect.

Action point 23
Reviewing perception

There is so much happening around us all the time which we fail to observe and use to our benefit. We are often so caught up in concerns about ourselves or the situation at the time that our seeking skills are low.

Think about the last conversation you had with a friend. Write down a summary of what was said, in as much detail as possible. Add any other aspect of the conversation, such as the gestures used by your friend; how did he look; what expressions were on his face? Now take the opportunity to ask for feedback on your friend's perception of the conversation and compare it with your own. You may be surprised by the fact that you each have different views of what took place.

Whether the differences are minor or major, they will affect your understanding of the conversation's message to some degree. The less effective an observer you are, the more distorted your understanding of the meeting. This, in turn, means that your reception of knowledge could be highly suspect and will distort any further feedback on yourself. The process of listening to and hearing what others say is more difficult than most of us believe. You will need to work hard at listening to and understanding the messages others are transmitting. This skill can be developed once you are aware of the need and adopt an interested and open attitude when dealing with others. Your mind has the capacity to think over four times faster than you can talk, so there is more than adequate capacity for you to receive and consider what another person says.

Your understanding will also be increased if you

take the trouble to check what the other person meant by the communication. Like most of us you may accept at face value what is said. Yet if you reflect on some of your recent conversations, you will probably realize that you did not communicate what you really felt and, like the majority of people, disguised your feelings because of the pressures or demands of the situation. We seldom communicate exactly what we intend because of various reasons which have built up into a complex pattern influencing us.

Let us look at some of the factors which influence us when we attempt to communicate with others. We start with an idea, message, or request which we want to give or receive. Most of us just slip into communicating this in an accidental and often casual and unprepared state. This being the case, it is easy to understand how other factors influence us and distort the message. The communication would be more effective if we thought in detail how we would transmit or receive the message to achieve maximum understanding.

The effectiveness of a communication can be influenced by the circumstances surrounding the exchange, the time of day or night, how alert or fatigued we are, whether we feel emotionally stable or unstable, whether we like or dislike the person, why the meeting is being held and how important achieving the objective is to us. The list could go on and on. The number of external and internal factors which affect us and impinge upon our thought process is considerable. Yet we have the power to control many of the factors by accepting responsibility for the communication. We can plan, evaluate, and achieve an effective level of understanding if we engage our minds to do so. The saying 'engage your brain before your mouth' is very apt.

The thinking process

How we think involves a complex process which is difficult to comprehend. Yet through practice we can achieve significant improvements. Most of us are trained to think logically from early youth. We are encouraged to believe that events happen in sequential order and in a logical way. This process of thinking can be supported by many examples from everyday life. You know the procedures used to boil water in an electric kettle. List the steps, assuming the kettle is empty. Now add a few contingencies; for example, what to do on completion of the operation if the water has not heated. In most cases you would check to find the fault and, again, a check list could be prepared. In the event that the fault was a lack of power, how would you boil the water? You may have difficulty in generating many solutions to the problem because you approached it as a logical thinker. This means that you were constrained within rigid boundaries to find a solution. We should not limit our capacity to solve problems by building a block to thinking by being only logical rather than also creative or lateral in our thinking process.

Brainstorming is a technique used to help problem-solving. A problem is considered from a basis of suggesting as many solutions as possible in a one or two minute session. It does not matter how ridiculous the suggestions are as they may contain the basis of a unique solution. All forms of evaluative judgement are suspended until all the possible solutions are presented in the time available.

You can use similar techniques every day: break out and become more creative in your thinking to provide a rich source of solutions for the problems which will confront you. Do not expect that every problem will be solved in a similar manner and thereby fail to consider the uniqueness of today's problems, coupled with the whole range of possible solutions using today's technology and resources.

By developing your thinking process you will soon discover that most things can be done if you really want to do them.

Imagination and creativity

There is a part of our brain which plays a significant role in achieving what we want out of life. This is the part concerned with our imagination and it tends to be the least developed part of our thinking. As we progress through life after starting our formal education our mind is programmed to receive and store information, to reason, analyse and judge events and situations and to memorize facts or events. Very little time is spent on the creative development of our imagination.

It is useful to understand how our imagination works and to be aware of its potential positive and negative power.

Most of the problems we face today are lodged in our imagination. By acting negatively the imagination becomes congested by fear, doubt and worry and makes us feel very insecure, unhappy and eventually depressed. As we allow our mind to develop its negative thoughts our imagination then forces us to act in a strange way. It comes between us and our friends and relations and becomes the breeding ground for greed, envy, suspicion, jealousy and eventually hate. By letting your imagination run wild you can create a monster which will devour you as a person and destroy your life. That is the force of its negative power.

Alternatively, we have the opportunity to switch on its positive power and create a new and exciting life. Being aware of our imagination and recognizing that it can affect our emotions should help us keep it under control. A direct link exists from the imagination to the part of the brain which controls emotions. For example we can sense a feeling of fear or great excitement on the basis of just a thought entering our mind. Our imagination sends pictures to the part of the brain which acts as our emotion control centre. This in turn, affects the feelings and functions of the body which multiplies the experience out of all context of reality. Negative reactions can be replaced with positive ones if you control your mind.

If we focus a little more on the imagination we can discover that it has several parts which are all powerful tools for creating a positive person.

The creative imagination

This part of the mind can generate ideas which form the creative response to your thoughts. All that we achieve can be related to the ideas sparked off by our creative imagination. Its dynamic power can provide many solutions to the problems and opportunities we face day by day. We can use our creative imagination to help us become self starters and achievers. Its power rests in our use of it to create a purposeful environment for us to grow and develop as thinking people.

The visual imagination

We use our visual imagination to create our self-image. We build pictures of ourselves from the information received and perceived. The power is again two-edged if taken to the extremes by our positive or negative selves. However we can use our visual imagination to build pictures, reconstruct and process in a useful way the constant flow of data we receive. We can use the feedback we receive in a powerful way to help us build a good visual picture of ourselves and of others.

The anticipative imagination

This relates to the part of the mind which looks ahead, plans, forecasts and anticipates. Once again its negative power can paralyse a person who anticipates that something dreadful will happen, whereas one can be energized by the excitement and expectation of anticipating something really good.

If you bring together and develop all the parts of the imagination and channel them in a positive way the result will be exciting. You will be able to project your future self onto the screen of your mind and let your positive imagination help you achieve it in reality. Your imagination can be used in helping others as you develop empathy with them.

By developing your mind you will also begin to develop your natural creativity. Education systems tend to dull our natural spirit of creativity to the point where it may be lost. Indeed, the process often starts before school with our parents adversely influencing us from the time we are very young. Unless our parents allow us the freedom to experiment and be creative, we soon learn to conform. The pressure on children to conform to 'normal' behaviour standards can be considerable and this in turn tends to suppress the natural desire for discovery and creativity. The imagination of a child using everyday kitchen implements to create his or her own world of reality is amazing and a pleasure to observe. Yet we possess the same imagination and ability to be creative and should encourage their use and development at every opportunity.

Action point 24
Creative thinking

> Select one of the following objects–paper clip, coat-hanger, comb, knife, fork, or cup. Now set aside two minutes to list all the uses you can think of for the chosen item. In a good session you should be able to list about 30 or 40 items.

You may have managed less than 20 uses and experienced difficulty in generating ideas. If you study your list, how many of the uses could be termed unusual and do not relate to a known or predictable use?

The basic problem stems from the fact that our creative instincts are often suppressed from early childhood. Our behavioural conditioning trains us to act and react in predictable and logical ways.

There can be great satisfaction gained from solving a problem by drawing on ideas from outside your normal thinking. You can develop your creativity by using the brainstorming technique to unlock new potential solutions to problems or opportunities which face you. Creativity is linked to the way you think and how you approach problem solving generally.

Solution seeking

It is important to emphasize the value of thinking positively in all that you do. It is rare to meet people who are positive thinkers. Yet each of us can become a person whose approach to life is from the positive mode. That kind of person stands out when the world seems dull and uninteresting. You may feel that you and many others are positive and approach life with optimism. Alternatively, you may feel that positive thinkers are people who view life through 'rose-tinted spectacles'.

Action point 25
Finding solutions

Consider the last problem you were confronted with in your life.

1 Write down what your first reactions and thoughts were. Now describe how you approached finding a solution and how in fact you resolved the problem (or did not).
2 Now consider the last opportunity you were offered and write down what were your thoughts and reactions to it. Describe how you approached the opportunity and the steps you took to realize or reject it.

Most people spend too much time identifying the difficulties and then stating them to others. Nearly all people are difficulty-staters when it comes to the process of solving problems or grasping opportunities. Listen to the next four people you meet and identify how many difficulties they face in their present life. Talk to someone who states that he intends to strive for some goal. Ask him to explain how he plans to achieve it and see how many problems and difficulties he states as opposed to solutions and opportunities.

Review your current attitude and approach to opportunities. You have the capacity to be a solution-seeker if you really want to. It is important to be creative in the process of seeking solutions because this can provide you with new opportunities. The difficulties which often confront you will assume a lesser dimension once you start trying to solve them creatively.

Action point 26
Brainstorming

> Return to Action point 25 and apply the brainstorming approach to both the problem and opportunity. Jot down ideas which could have been solutions. Allocate two minutes to each subject and try not to evaluate the answers. You could involve a friend or colleagues and form a brainstorming group. You may be surprised by the number of really exciting and positive solutions which are generated.

This positive attitude will help you to approach your goals with renewed vigour and enthusiasm knowing that you will turn any problems on the way into opportunities.

6 RELATIONSHIP SKILLS

Relating to others

We have a natural need to belong to some group of society. Since early days people have congregated in tribes or clans and built group relationships. Today we can observe the need felt by the majority to be part of a group. However, there will always appear to be some who do not like to be in groups but prefer to be 'loners'. The question is whether those people really do want to be alone. The following story by C J Wendel says much about relationships and the effect which others can have upon us.

The unmailed letter

Dear Teacher

Today at assembly we had a stimulating address, 'The Education I Wish I Might Have Had'. It made me think. And I'm going to break loose and tell you about memories some fellows have which I haven't had.

I wish I could remember one morning that you greeted me with a happy smile when I walked into the room. It would have made such a bright beginning for the day. I know that I wasn't much to look at with my brown freckled face crowned with a mop of red hair that just wouldn't stay down, no matter how often I combed it. And my ears – that's why they were always so dirty – they were so big, and they stuck straight out catching every particle of dirt that the wind swept by. My clothes were dirty too, but that wasn't altogether my fault. Mother never did feel well after baby Sally was born, and I could always dirty my clothes faster than she could get around to wash them. I can hear Mother say in her tired voice: 'Johnny, how do you ever get so dirty?' She promised me she would wash my trousers after I had gone to bed (I only had one pair), but I guess she was just too tired after putting Sally to bed. Then tucking in Billy and Bob, the twins, and Mary, Jane, Tommy and me for the night, before leaving to hunt for Dad who would be in any one of the six taverns. You can't imagine how much your smile would have meant on some of those mornings that I came to school with only a dry crust of bread for my breakfast. Once or twice I thought you were going to smile – and then, you just said in a stern voice: 'Johnny, you're late again – as usual'. That 'as usual' as an afterthought always cut like a knife, and that's why I was afraid you wouldn't understand if I told you the real reason why I was late. Baby Sally needed the milk, and I used to walk the three miles over to Smith's every morning and get it. He sold us the milk two cents cheaper than Mr Jones who lived just across the road from us.

I wish I could remember one kind word that you spoke to me directly, or one time when we played games that you joined the circle next to me and took my hand like you did the other boys'. True, my hands always looked dirty, it's hard to wash in cold well-water without soap, but if I'd known there was a chance that you would have taken hold of my hand, I'd have scrubbed until they had been clean. The only time you seemed to notice me was when I pulled Norma's hair or poked Mary with my pencil. No-one wanted to play with me, and sometimes I felt like I had to do something like that to make sure I was still alive.

I wish I could remember one time you included me in the planning of the class work, instead of simply ignoring me. I rebelled at that – not the work itself, as you supposed when I caused a disturbance or did everything except the work I was supposed to do – but because you didn't consider my views or reasons.

I wish I could remember, above all else, just one time that you and I talked together alone discussing my problems, so that you could have had a better understanding of why I had to do some of the things I did. It was always so easy for you to solve any problem that came up in class, and I'm sure that you could have helped me with my own problems and troubles.

Please do not think I am blaming you. No teacher could ever have worked harder and had the children's welfare more at heart than you did. No one could have taught me better how to work, or set a better example of honesty, industry and clean living. But you just didn't know that I, too, dirty and late as I was, needed those things that you have had with you all the time – things that you gave freely to others but withheld from me. You couldn't have been better to me – no teacher could – but surely you could have been infinitely nearer.

Your one-time pupil,

PS I can't send this. After all these years you wouldn't understand. But I wish you knew that I'd gladly give my four years of school for the memories I might have had.*

We are generally very fragile when it comes to

* LADANYE, Thomas W, ed. *Plain Talk*. Thomas W Ladanye, 1980.

human relationships. We become extra sensitive when we experience emotions such as fear, suspicion, hate, love and joy. This tends to make us vulnerable to the attentions of others. The need for security is high and it demands a great deal of effort from those involved to make a relationship work successfully.

As you develop a creative and positive solution seeking attitude, your sensitivity to others' needs will be heightened. You will endeavour to make each relationship work from a foundation of confidence and trust. As you make a genuine effort this will draw a similar response from others. They will not respond in the same way because they will react in relation to how you meet their needs, but you can be certain that the majority, if not all, will respond in kind.

Why we communicate

We communicate as a means of relating to others. Communication is as essential to relationships as food is to the body. Yet in the same way as we abuse our diet, we apply the same careless indifference to our communications. Where there is a lack of effective communication, this can often be traced to our childhood and early youth where we may not have been encouraged to listen and hear what others were saying and relate to them. Instead our learning was geared to receive information, record it, and to reproduce it in a competitive situation. We could then go through life with our blinkers on unaware of the real needs of the people with whom we came into contact.

Action point 27
Analysis of interaction

Think about the last time you felt dissatisfied with

the result of a conversation or meeting. What factors made you unhappy? List these and describe how they arose and what influenced your thinking.

Did you in the meeting describe how you felt or what in fact you expected from the interaction? If not, what reasons did you have for holding back?

How do you feel if a person, or group, responds to your communication in a way that fails to meet your needs at the time? Do you attempt to communicate your feelings as best you can or do you withhold them and fail to disclose your need of help and understanding? As it is not part of our culture to disclose our inner needs, many of your conversations and contributions will be at surface level with few being at a deeper level of feeling. That is unless you become emotional and react in terms of fear, anger, happiness or love. In that case, you will disclose your feelings to a degree dependent upon the emotional strength discharged at the time.

In most instances when you meet others, there is a genuine desire to be reasonably open and natural. You know how you feel at the time and can understand what your needs are and how these can be met. By being open, you can help others respond in a positive manner to satisfy your own needs. Correspondingly, because you understand your own felt needs, you should also be able to perceive the inner needs of others. If these are not clear under the protection of the façades being presented, you should still be able to get beneath the surface and discover their needs. This process requires understanding and trust in that you are being genuine in trying to achieve empathy with others. You will discover that by mentally 'putting yourself in others' shoes', you will gain a better understanding of their needs.

How we communicate

The communication process is an extremely complex one involving many different ways of achieving our purpose. The following simple model has been developed to illustrate some of the different stages in a verbal communication between two people.

First person

thinks about what he intends to say
says it
considers if that is what he meant to say
wonders what the other person heard and understood
waits for feedback to check understanding
receives the feedback and then thinks about what he intends to say in response

Second person

thinks about what is going to be said
listens to what is said
compares it with his understanding of the situation
compares it with the non-verbal signals present
thinks about what he will say in response, what impact he intends to have, and how it will affect the other person
says what he means to say
looks for the intended reaction and feedback
thinks about what he might say in response

Further stages could be added to each of the people involved to emphasize further the complexity of the process in comparison to the time taken for the conversation. The thinking and speaking process for each person is normally accomplished in a matter of seconds in a free-flowing conversation.

Action point 28
Process of meetings

Reflect back to Action point 27 and compare the communication with the above model. Does it now provide you with some answers as to why you and others did not achieve the necessary level of understanding? Think about how you could have changed the meeting process to have made it work more effectively.

The power of the mind is such that it can accomplish a great deal in a short space of time. We have the potential to achieve more efficient communication through effectively harnessing this power.

Verbal communication

This is often thought of as the easiest part of communication: you think about what you want to say, draw from a reservoir of words, and then speak. The other person will receive them and a similar process commences. This simplistic view is far from the truth, as you will know from your own experience. In the first instance, although we may use the same words as others, they often do not mean the same thing to them. For example, if you look at the word FAIR in the dictionary, you will discover that it has many meanings, including the following:

meeting place for shows and games
sale of goods
pleasant weather
colour of hair
beautiful woman
satisfactory
complexion

unblemished face
above board

Action point 29
Meaning of words

Write down as many meanings for the following words as you can think of

fast
success
aware
being

Compare your responses with a dictionary.

This emphasizes the importance of choosing and using words. Your sentence structure clarifies the meaning of the words you use. You select the appropriate words, and structure how they are spoken, to ensure that the message will communicate what you intend. This provides you with the opportunity to check understanding when the response is received. You will be able to communicate more effectively as your awareness of the importance of the selection and use of words increases.

In the second instance we focus on the way we say the word. We naturally use different intonations of voice when we speak and this places special emphasis upon the meaning we place on particular words. Our intonation defines the meaning we intend to transmit and can change the literal meaning of the words used. If you consider the word FUNNY and define it to mean something amusing to you, then apply intonation as follows:

That's funny	It amuses you
That's funny . . .	There is something puzzling you

THAT'S funny?	You are not amused
He is a funny person	He is amusing you
He is a 'funny' person	There is something peculiar about him
He *IS* a funny person	You do not understand him or his behaviour

To read the statements without an understanding of where the intonation lies would make each come across as meaning the same. This example also highlights the difficulty of expressing effectively in writing how intonation changes meaning. The power to use intonation to be precise in communicating your ideas is an exciting one.

The skill of voice modulation is taught very early in life and is reinforced as you grow. The development of a child and parent relationship clearly illustrates the use of voice modulation. When a mother or father is projecting love and affection, the voice is soft and full of attention. When projecting anger the voice is shrill and critical. One of the most common words used is 'don't'. In the early stages of its use with young children, it can be said in a quiet and loving way to show concern for the safety of the child. As the word becomes a command (which can still be based on love and concern) it assumes a much louder and more critical tone. If the parent is pushed further, it develops into a hysterical shout which portrays the anger and frustration felt and can reflect lack of control over the situation. We progress through various stages of loudness based upon the belief that the louder we shout, the better we communicate our commands. In reality, the opposite is normally achieved.

The negative side of how we react has been emphasized because most people appear to relate this more easily to their experience. However, the purpose is to illustrate how we use modulations of our voice to convey special feelings and intentions.

It is just as appropriate when we are operating in a positive way to project our feelings through our voice modulation. Therefore, if you want to help someone else understand what you are saying, it is essential that you select and say the words in a precise way to communicate your meaning. This will be on two levels, with the first being the factual level and the second being the feeling level.

To achieve communication on a factual level you will select those words which most clearly describe the idea, situation, or message you are attempting to send. You will be careful to choose words which readily describe, and those which support the message in a way which aids understanding.

It is certainly possible to reach the necessary understanding by communicating with people on only the factual level. When you add the feeling level, you then enter the emotional arena and this is where you can find the greatest satisfaction – and experience the most difficulty.

When communicating feelings, it is important for you to be genuine and not cloud the message. If you are projecting one thing while you think something quite different, the results will be unclear, although other behaviour may give a better indication of your true feelings.

Non-verbal communication

Scientists state that we say more about ourselves,

and of what we are thinking, through our non-verbal signals. We cannot stop ourselves, in many instances, from transmitting the signals of what we really are, and think at any time. We send signals about ourselves in a whole range of different ways, which include the following:

Through the face

the way we look, use our mouth, tongue and lips
our eyes, and what they say when we link them to our eyebrows
our expressions portraying how we feel

Our posture

the way we approach others
the way we stand, walk and run
the expressions projected through body posture
how we present ourselves

Our hands

how we greet others
how we shake hands
how we express points with our hands
whether they are rough or smooth

There are many ways in which we communicate to others what and who we are.

Action point 30
Communicating with others

List all the ways you communicate with others. Think about how you deal with family, close friends, colleagues, boss or subordinates and the people with whom you do not get on. Describe the differences and the reasons why you deal with them in different ways.

You will probably be surprised by the number of different ways you project yourself to others. This brings us back to the point made earlier about distortion of the message. If you are saying in words something which is not supported by your non-verbal behaviour, the receiver will be confused. However low your self-awareness may be, you will still be perceptive or intuitive enough to spot this. You have an inbuilt system which identifies to some degree when people are not being honest with you.

How feedback works

To know ourselves fully, we need to know others. This is because we need to relate to others to enable our inner needs to be satisfied. To gain a greater awareness of yourself, it was earlier suggested that you should attempt the action points and check how your perception compared with someone else's perception of you. With the extra dimension of the ideas covered in this chapter added to the picture you built previously, you should become aware of the significance of your relationships with others.

Now you are thinking more carefully about the words you use, are aware of how you say them, and have an increased understanding of the role of non-verbal communication. The vital element which reality plays in the feedback process will be clearer to you. To make an analogy, to take a good photograph of yourself you need to ensure that everything is set up correctly to take the picture. Should the camera be faulty, or the lens out of focus, or the film damaged, or the light inadequate, or a combination of these or any other factors, the resulting picture will not be a true image.

To receive effective feedback, you will need to ask the correct questions and set the scene as previously described. This involves a great deal of thinking about what you really want from the feedback. If it is ego strokes or compliments you want, you can structure your activities to ensure that people will provide the necessary strokes. On the other hand, if you prefer to collect negative strokes, you will lead a life which creates the necessary reaction. You have the power to decide what you want to be. You will effectively progress towards this if you project yourself and seek honest feedback on which to develop.

Action point 31
Effective interaction

1 Refer to Action points 27, 28, and 30 and check whether you stated your views in the most effective manner. Check that you used words which truly described what you felt and believed about your self. Now think about how you asked for the feedback. What did you feel at the time? Were you surprised by what was said? How did you react? Were you emotional about the disclosures?
2 Plan how you might now change the words and ideas set out in the action points mentioned above. Also plan how you would now approach a feedback session. Try out your plan and compare the sessions to determine the benefits to be derived from an honest transaction.

It is important to continue to brief others where appropriate if you wish to gain maximum benefit from a feedback session. However, you can gain just as much feedback from others you relate to who are not aware of your self-development plan. As you progress through life and interact with others, they are constantly sending you feedback signals, either of the verbal or non-verbal kind. Whichever way they are transmitted, you should be alert and ready to receive them. The more aware you become, the more you will perceive the vast amount of feedback which is continuously being given – even when a direct interaction is not involved. Think about the most recent time you were invited to a function which involved a number of people. Consider how many people you tried to interest or impress during the evening? How did you attract their attention? What behaviours did you use? You can achieve a great deal of feedback by observing others react to your presence. You can develop the range of your feedback by being aware that it can be obtained through any situation.

Action point 32
Feedback sessions

1 List where you think you could receive feedback on yourself outside an organized feedback session. Also list how you might be able to identify the feedback and what you will have to do to create the necessary conditions.
2 Try out some of the ideas in a variety of situations and observe the results.

The more you actively review feedback from all sources, the more you will understand yourself and others.

Returning to the analogy of the camera: if you are using an automatic camera, then the camera will determine the focus, light reading and other factors to produce a perfect picture. However, it still depends upon the person to decide in which direction to point the camera. In a similar way you can use your level of self-awareness and understanding together with the feedback you receive to arrive at a clear picture of yourself. You can then decide in which direction you want to go with your relationships and your life.

One to one relationships

Most of your life is comprised of one to one relationships, whether they be at work, home, education, community, or leisure. If you analyse group activities, you will be able to identify how often these break down into a series of one to one interactions. The major benefit to be gained from single, as against multiple, relationships is the depth of understanding which can be developed.

We can illustrate the danger which faces many relationships by looking at the following. Two people meet, begin to interact with each other and the relationship develops. The couple spend a great deal of time together, but without really getting to know each other because there is a real fear, felt by both sides, that any disclosure of themselves might adversely affect the relationship. They tend to present their best side to the other. Once they live together, the façades come down and they begin to see each other as they really are. Some partners may have noticed faults earlier in the relationship but believed that they could change the other person. The result could be a less than happy and meaningful relationship in the long term.

The opportunity to use time constructively throughout a relationship is valuable as it provides an ideal opportunity to experience a real understanding of someone else and for you to discover more about yourself. Although a bleak picture has been painted above, it tends to reflect very accurately what happens to many one to one relationships. Happily, however, there are many others which do achieve the depth of understanding between the partners which ensures a long and satisfactory relationship.

Lack of honesty in a relationship is the main cause of its eventual failure. Unless built upon openness and trust, a relationship cannot grow and develop. The three stages in a relationship, opening, developing and closing will now be explored.

Opening a relationship

How do you go about opening a relationship with another person?

Action point 33
Starting a relationship

> Describe how you would go about opening a relationship with a person who you want to be a friend. Compare this with how you would go about getting to know a person with whom you want to be 'more than just good friends'.

How did you plan to start the 'getting acquainted' stage? What did you plan to disclose about your interest and intentions? What would you disclose about yourself? These and many other questions could be asked. We tend to operate from different levels in our relationships and these are as follows:

Level 1:
This is the getting acquainted small talk which is just better than the embarrassing silence which often accompanies the opening of a relationship. However it does act as an 'ice breaker' and can catch the other person's interest.

Level 2:
This is when you discuss something you or others have done. Here you are still talking about what you have done and who you know. There is no disclosure about you, the person.

Level 3:
You are now prepared to risk some disclosure abut yourself – your ideas, opinions, beliefs and attitudes. You will probably be cautious about this stage and at the first sign of rejection, you will retreat to the first two levels.

Level 4:
You have reached the point where you allow your emotion to come to the fore. Your feelings are communicated to the other person and you begin to understand each other. The risk at this stage is that you might be hurt or become euphoric, and your behaviour makes you vulnerable if there is over reaction one way or the other. If you receive adverse results at this level, you will certainly regress and it will take a long time before you expose yourself to similar risks. However, assuming a positive result you can achieve the peak of interpersonal relationships at the next level.

Level 5:
You are comfortable to talk honestly about yourself and how you feel and who you are. You are legitimate or genuine with others and are courageous in disclosing yourself. You build on a basis of trust because, as you learn about others, you will learn about yourself. The others, in turn, will also learn about themselves in a positive and non-threatening way.

Action point 34
Your level of interaction

What levels would you use to open a relationship with:

(a) a member of the opposite sex?
(b) a stranger from another country?
(c) a well respected person of authority?

Developing relationships

One of the major stumbling blocks in developing a meaningful relationship is the question of ownership. This can result in unhealthy behaviours such as fear, jealousy, anger, concern, rigidity and suspicion which feed and grow and make the relationship insecure.

If you are prepared to aim for the legitimate level in each of your relationships, this will provide the other person with a clear picture of you and your aspirations. As the relationship develops, the understanding between you will sharpen and this will enable each of you to help the other to achieve fulfilment through self-confidence and inner strength. By becoming a thoughtful person, you are now able to relate on a legitimate basis to all those with whom you come in contact.

As you experiment with various levels you will discover that others will respond in a similar way. Some may decide to take advantage of you, but these people will assume a very limited role in your future life. The strength to be open and honest, without hurting others, will grow daily until you feel confident to face everyone in a positive way. The stages used to reach the peak level may take time and they should not be rushed. Your awareness will act as a sensor and tell you, from the feedback, when to proceed to higher levels.

The ultimate level provides a fertile field for growth of yourself and others. The freedom you feel will be based upon a high degree of self-discipline and responsibility for others. This will guide your development in the most productive way and will allow feedback on the highest level.

It is at this point where different needs could see the strength of a relationship change. Those involved may find that the joy and benefits derived from the relationship are no longer achieved. This is facing the reality of life in that we do change as people and develop new needs which require to be fulfilled through other relationships.

Changing and closing relationships

It is sad when a close and productive relationship ends. This is heightened when it ends in acrimony for one or both of the people involved. There is no need for this to happen if the relationship has been built on the basis of legitimacy.

Action point 35
Changing relationships

Describe how you would end a relationship which was built upon a legitimate foundation.

The process of ending a relationship is easy if you have developed a level of trust and openness in which you will both be aware of changing circumstances. The joy of a true relationship depends upon the degree to which you are in tune with each other. Changes by you or your partner will be sensed and brought out in an open way for discussion. Once the facts and feelings have been disclosed, you will both decide upon the best course of action. There is every chance that the relationship will continue in a different way to meet the changed circumstances. These is no need for the relationship to be completely destroyed.

A legitimate relationship will survive and continue though it may pass through various stages. The people concerned will respond to each other's needs in a responsible way and allow each other the freedom to develop. However, it takes a great deal of selflessness to help others and it may hurt. The reward is in seeing each other grow and in developing new relationships.

Equipped with a sound framework for developing one to one relationships you will then obtain much more benefit from group relationships.

Group relationships

We spend a great deal of our time with various groups of people. Whether this be at home, education, work, community or during our leisure activities we seem to be in groups. This meets our need to belong and be part of an activity but we seldom seem to get as much out of our involvement as we could. A great deal happens in groups which influences how much each person gives and receives from the experience. The complexities of the communication process were described earlier; what happens in groups is every bit as complex.

Group dynamics is a term used to describe the interplay which takes place in every group. There will be various levels of motivation and interest contributed by those involved. This will then reflect the level of energy applied by each to make the group work and achieve what it was set up to do. However homogeneous or disparate the people in the group are, group dynamics will exist to some degree. It is therefore valuable to understand what is going on and who is attempting what in the process. Two main aspects of group work are now considered.

First, there needs to be a purpose or task to achieve which brings the people together into the group. Secondly, there is the interaction between the people which results in the task being accomplished or not, and this is known as the process. It refers to how people work together as opposed to what they do to accomplish the task. This is explained further when the roles people adopt in groups are considered.

Group roles: Each one of us adopts at least one role, and probably several roles, in each group. These roles vary from providing leadership to that of support. Although we can perform very positive roles, it is just as likely for negative roles to appear. It depends upon the attitude adopted by each person and the objectives they set in terms of what they intend to contribute to, or take from, the group.

You can obtain much more satisfaction and achieve effectiveness if you are aware of the roles you and others adopt.

Action point 36
Contribution to groups

Note the last three group events in which you were involved. Describe the contribution or deduction you made to help or hinder the group achieve its goals. Think of how you felt at the time and what motivated you to act in the way you did. Describe what you could now do to be more effective in helping the group.

The following are the main group roles. There are an enormous number of variations to reflect individual contributions but they nearly all stem from six basic roles.

Leader

This is the person who provides the drive and direction to mould a group of people to achieve their goals. Leaders operate from four main styles of 'tell', 'sell', 'consult', and 'participate'.

(a) The 'tell' leader gets things done by being completely directive in marshalling those in the group. There is authority and control with very limited discussion about what should be done. The 'tell' leader may often take on a major portion of the work in order to get it done because others are not achieving as quickly as the leader requires.

(b) The 'sell' leader uses a great deal of persuasion to get the group to do what the leader wants. The 'sell' leader is very like the 'tell' leader, except for the need to convince people that they should do it the leader's way because that is the best.

The 'sell' leader tends to be less autocratic and demanding but still wants the task done his way.

(c) The 'consult' leader involves the group in discussing the best ways to achieve their goals. This leader has thought it out and has formed plans but is prepared to check these with the group. When the group inputs ideas which are consistent with the leader's plan, they will be readily adopted. However, if they radically change the plan, and the leader does not like them, they may not be adopted.

(d) The 'participative' leader involves the group in the total process of planning and deciding on the goals and how they will be realized. Meetings will be run on democratic lines and all decisions will be arrived at by means of consensus. The main objective of the participative leader is to involve all members of the group in the whole process to ensure their full commitment to agreed objectives.

You may be able to identify other variations to the four styles, or, in fact, discover other styles. It does not matter as long as you are consistent in the use of styles and understand how each operates. You can develop a simple matrix of leadership styles and the way they operate with others and this could be a useful checklist for your future analysis.

The main point to remember is that leaders in their different styles are usually effective in achieving what they set out to do and may vary according to the task. Another point to note is that the actual leader of a group may not be the appointed or elected leader. This often happens and should not affect the performance of the group as long as there is no conflict between the leaders.

Leadership comes in many forms and may cover an extended period or a very short time. Groups are dynamic and there are constant demands for leadership of different kinds during the activity. You can have an elected leader providing the formal chairing role with other group members providing relevant leadership roles.

Action point 37
Leadership roles

Turn to your last action point and identify any leadership roles you adopted during the three group activities. Describe what you did and what mix of styles you adopted.

Supporters

These are the backbone of the group and are the people who supply the support and energy to accomplish the given task.

Supporters are positive assets to any group because they are in tune with what is required and are motivated to get it done. You will find that to achieve results, you will need a quota of supporters. They are not, as often thought, 'yes' people who readily agree with every idea, even if the ideas oppose each other. Supporters are people who get a great deal of enjoyment and satisfaction from being involved in the 'hands on' part of group work. Provide them with a mission and they will willingly work to accomplish the task successfully. The supporters will provide the necessary back-up to enable the leadership to operate effectively. With ineffective leadership, you will discover that supporters' efforts will diminish before they find a new leader.

Builders

These are people who are normally closely associated with leaders. They can see the objectives and have a capacity to project ideas which improve the plans. Builders also help to create the conditions which enable the group to gel and work in harmony. The builder looks for ways to make the task easier as well as cement good relationships. In group dynamic terms the builder is concerned with both the task and the process, whereas the supporter is mainly concerned with the task.

Innovators

They introduce creativity into the group and enable it to achieve its goals more effectively. They are usually people who are able to think clearly and can see the wood for the trees. They are not necessarily locked into the task as 'hands on' people, but are more distant and abstract about the project. This can make them appear self-contained and possibly not good mixers. However, there are many innovators who are the 'life and soul of the party' and they use this as a way of introducing their ideas. If the idea is picked up and acted upon, they feel good; on the other hand, if it is rejected, the jocular style will hide any hurt they may feel. Once again, anyone can be the innovator, as we all have the potential to be creative.

Jesters

They are the few people in a group who keep the others amused, particularly when the going is rough. Groups are able to pass through very tough times with the aid of a jester. They add the laughter and amuse the members in a balanced and effective way. The jester tends to be an extroverted person who is not afraid of making an exhibition of himself. The jester's sensitivity to the needs of the group is high and contributions are made when required. This is one role which many group members would feel incapable of doing. Yet most members will inject humour into the group at times. The main distinction between members and jesters is that the jester is seen as a 'character' by the members.

Administrators

These people provide the flow of information and attend to the needs of the group to help it achieve. There is always someone who acts as secretary, treasurer, or organizer and ensures that the timetable, paperwork, and arrangements are organized correctly. The administrator is an essential member of the team and provides the framework around which the others build. They are often identified as the academic, retired, or quiet members of the group. However, this role cold be undertaken by most members. It does need a precise and clear thinking person who feels inclined to help the process whereby the others will get the task accomplished.

Action point 38
Your role in groups

Turn back to Action point 36 and consider the roles you adopted in the three events. Count the number of times you used the roles and this will give you some idea of your preferred styles in each event. You should also now consider how you will operate in future groups to help them achieve their results.

By increasing your awareness of what is happening in groups, you will be able to make a better contribution to their effectiveness. You will also have realized that most groups need at least one of each role to be performed to help it work well. This does not mean that you will need six people in each group. There is no guarantee that the six could adopt the separate roles anyway. What can happen is for one person to be able to adopt several roles during the event. If this is done with understanding of what the group needs, it will be valuable to the other members.

You will probably be able to identify multiple roles which you use in groups. Take time to develop these and add others which you believe you can usefully use. The outcome will be positive for yourself and the group as you will be sensitive to both your own and the group's needs. This will then enable you to adopt the most useful role to help the group push forward in harmony. When others are also aware of group roles, the resources of the group can then be channelled in a much more effective manner.

How to help people

This is one of the most difficult, yet exciting, topics. Most of us are keen to be regarded as people others come to for advice and guidance. There is great personal satisfaction to be gained from being in a position to influence others.

You should avoid the dangerous trap of believing that you have some great gift, or that you must guide others from your base of knowledge or experience. There are many people who will seek advice and guidance on what they should do in any and every situation. The temptation to give advice should be tempered with the realization that it may not be in the best interest for that person. The harm and de-motivation which could result from a person following your advice, if it were wrong, is too great a risk to take. It is much better to influence the person by helping him to help himself. Chapter 9 discusses counselling and coaching as a process of helping ourselves and others to be effective. By following that process, each person is more likely to achieve their goals and resolve difficulties satisfactorily. In the end, by helping others to solve their own problems, you will help them develop and gain more self respect than if you have influenced them to accept your own ready made solution to their problem.

By providing positive help you will develop trusting relationships which will enable you to influence others. This influence will be more in terms of the process they use to solve their problems than in telling them what to do.

How to achieve results through others

This is the role which most managers have in the organization of their jobs. Yet the task is generally handled in a very unsatisfactory way. People are often seen as units of production and not given the level of involvement which could result in higher productivity. Most of us would work better if we understood what happened to the effort we contributed to the product or service. Given the opportunity we could apply energy, potential and creativity to make our job much more interesting and effective.

Action point 39
Achieving results through others

> Having studied this chapter, and drawing from your increasing self-awareness, list the factors which would enable you to achieve results through others. Describe how you plan to use these to help you achieve.

You will probably include in your list such factors as involvement, commitment, trust, defined objectives, motivation and leadership. It is clear that people will work effectively if they are given the purpose, understanding and tools to do whatever job is at hand. They will also need to feel committed and this can be achieved through involvement. If you treat people with trust and dignity, they will respond.

This process also applies to your quest for self-development. If you help people to help you and set the ground rules well, they will respond in a positive manner. You will need to develop trust, and let them see that you are being legitimate in your desire for their help. You will receive it without obligation and it will help others to start thinking about helping themselves.

7 SITUATIONAL SKILLS

Learning from experience

The last two chapters demonstrated the wide range of individual and group skills which can be acquired and the equally wide range of situations in which these skills can be used. The next step is to learn how to apply and develop these skills in particular situations and to use the feedback received to achieve the desired results. Experiential learning helps you identify positive skills and reinforce them in each new situation; it also helps to identify those which are less effective and enables you to improve them.

Life provides us all with excellent possibilities for learning about ourselves and others. As we engage in an interaction or event, we are provided with an opportunity to learn. How much we learn is dependent upon our level of awareness and motivation. With an increasing level of both, we can gain much from life's experiences.

The purpose of this chapter is to raise your level of awareness of the skills required and knowledge of when to use them.

Personal characteristics required

Personal characteristics have been discussed in the

earlier chapters as they related to individual or relationship skills. Most of these also apply to situational skills and the following is a description of the most significant ones.

Openness

Keep an open mind and carefully consider each event and idea to obtain the best results from it. Some people have a tendency to relate the present to the past. They evaluate the present using the criteria of the past without making the necessary allowances for changed circumstances, people, technology or any other factors. You will hear of decisions made on the basis, 'We can't do that because we tried it before and it didn't work'. New attempts are therefore discounted even before the full facts are considered.

If you keep an open mind, consider all new ideas, and think through the different opinions offered, you give yourself a better chance of learning and making better decisions.

Awareness

This applies both to self-awareness and awareness about others. If you develop a conscious sensitivity to yourself and others, it will enable you to deal with situations in an effective way. This will help others gain in confidence because you will be able to meet their needs, and they will relate better to you. This in turn means that the feedback will be better.

Flexibility

Be adaptable to the needs of the situation and of the people involved. An awareness of what is happening in situations will give you the flexibility to adapt your position to achieve positive results.

Communications
The importance of communicating your ideas and instructions in a precise manner was discussed earlier. In each situation the open and aware person will be able to produce a high level of communication which will result in clearer and more helpful interaction and feedback.

Analytical
The ability to consider each situation and size it up quickly is of immense value. You should use this ability in your approach to problem solving and the use of your solution seeking skills to reach effective answers. To be able to stand back from the problem and observe the influencing factors can help you take an objective view.

Empathy
To be concerned about others will help you gain better insights into people's various circumstances.

Others will sense your awareness and will develop a basis of trust and understanding. They will be more open and honest with you, and prepared to challenge you in a constructive way. Objective feedback will be increased and this will provide you with greater self-awareness.

Creativity
The more able you are to respond with resourcefulness to people and events, the greater will be your self-learning. Each situation will provide you with the opportunity to be innovative and allow your imagination to work.

Action point 40
Personal characteristics

List the personal characteristics which would help you to learn most from each separate event in your life. Describe how these characteristics could help you.

How does your list compare with the above characteristics? Were you able to relate the individual and relationship skills described in the previous sections to situations?

Co-ordinating skills

Co-ordinating skills involves a process whereby your individual skills are brought to bear on relationships in every situation. As your skill increases and you develop a heightened self-awareness, you will then be able to use this in a variety of situations.

Action point 41
Influencing situations

Think about three recent situations where the characteristics you used influenced the result. List how each one contributed and if the result was less than you expected, why did this happen and how could you have changed course to have achieved your expectations?

When you become involved in a situation, it places a number of demands upon you. The level of demand will be in direct proportion to the support you need from other people to achieve your goals and your level of involvement. Even if only a casual bystander you can still be drawn into the event to give an opinion, settle an argument or provide feedback. You can also remain uninvolved outwardly whilst at the same time you may wish inwardly to be involved.

If you wish to obtain maximum value from each event, you will be required to give it your undivided attention. You will need to be actively involved in whatever decision is reached, and be committed to its achievement. When difficulties are encountered you help others to resolve conflict, reduce stress, achieve understanding and move on to reach a consensus decision.

Action point 42
Analysis of impact

1 Refer to two encounters in the past where you felt that you could have contributed more effectively. Think about what held you back and could have been achieved if you had become more involved.
2 What could you have done to make your contribution have the impact you wished?
3 Relate your answers to those individual and relationship skills which would help you to overcome the difficulties.

You may have noted that you were afraid of being seen as foolish, or not being respected enough to add your comments. There are many reasons why we do not become involved when we feel we should. By assessing these and relating them to individual and relationship skills, you can identify how to become more effective. We usually want to get the best out of each situation, and methods of doing this will become clearer as you progress.

Learning from situations

Each situation can provide you with an ideal opportunity to learn about yourself and others. You will be able to reach a stage where a great deal of enjoyment and satisfaction can be obtained from each event. This is not restricted to fun events – similar feelings can be obtained from a whole range of situations at home, education, work, in the community and from leisure.

Your approach to a tense and conflict-loaded meeting should be structured to enable you to play a positive and constructive role. You should aim to ease the event to a satisfactory stage where, at least, the problems or opportunities have been identified. Each stage beyond that would be a bonus until real consensus resulted in full commitment to whatever course of action was decided. When the situation is informal and there is no need to decide on a course of action, the same responsibility rests with you and the others to help it achieve the most satisfactory end.

When you know what you expect from a situation and achieve this, you are then in a position to look at the part you played in the process of achievement. The feedback obtained from this is very useful for your future development. The more you are aware of what is happening in situations the better equipped you will be to take advantage of each opportunity.

Action point 43
Improving understanding

1 In what ways could you improve your understanding of what is happening in each situation? How do you identify what each person involved is trying to achieve?
2 Can you separate what you want and are prepared to disclose from what you want but feel unable to disclose?

Focus on meetings

A meeting can be defined as an event where two or more meet together for some purpose. If we understand who is involved and what they are trying to achieve, this provides us with a better basis to assist the meeting achieve its purpose.

Being aware of the significance of each meeting will help you to be prepared with your defined objective. This will place you in a strong position to achieve the best possible result from the meeting. Irrespective of the purpose of the meeting, you can determine what you want to achieve from it. You can consider the limits you would place on variations to your objectives and if the meeting is a negotiation define clearly where you may concede on some issues to gain on others. In addition, by knowing what you want to achieve, you will be able to utilize fully the process of any meeting.

It is important to establish and agree the ground rules under which the meeting will be conducted. Establishing this element of the process is vital to ensure that both parties understand at the beginning their relative positions. If you reflect on your two most recent meetings and think about what happened you should be able to identify the rules which applied.

Let us turn our attention to each area of our lives and look at some of the people we meet and interact with:

Home

Parents; brothers and sisters; relatives; friends; neighbours; local, regional and national government agencies.

Education
Head teacher; principal teachers; teachers; friends; colleagues; inspectors; student teachers; guidance counsellors; tutors; professors; lecturers.

Work
Friends; colleagues; supervisors; peers; subordinates; managers; union representatives; specialists; clients; suppliers; visitors.

Community
Public servants; specialists; friends; neighbours; parents; colleagues; relatives.

Leisure
Any of the people listed above, plus instructors who teach us skills.

In the course of living we meet a great number of people from all aspects of life. You can choose who you want to relate to and there are others who will come into contact with you without your choosing. Some will want to make contact with you as they may wish you to help them achieve their objectives.

The main point is that you should approach each event with a positive attitude and with the aim of achieving the most out of the meeting.

Types of meeting

There are as many types of meeting as there are groups who meet. Each group is unique because of the mix of people and the objectives of the meetings. Even when the same group of people stop a discussion to reconvene later, the subsequent meeting will be different. However, there are ways of categorizing meetings which may be of help. The following category system is only a rough guide designed to help you relate to the events. As your awareness increases, you may develop your own categories to meet your needs.

Action point 44
Purposes of meetings

> Cast your mind back over the last three months and list the meetings you attended. Describe the purpose of each meeting. Is there a pattern emerging which would enable you to relate to each type of meeting? If you have identified a pattern, list each type, and give it a one word description which is meaningful to you.

The objective in this section is to interpret the meeting to enable you to contribute positively; included are the face to face, the small group and the large gathering. You will achieve more from the meeting if you ascertain others' needs and attempt to meet these in some way. The following can form a basis for the development of your own categories.

1 Friendly
A friendly meeting is defined as one where the participants relate well to each other and have the common objective of really enjoying themselves. This could be no more than a casual conversation to no less than a full-blown and wild party.

In friendly meetings you feel free enough to be yourself, to be relaxed and to react and respond in a natural way. You will find that very little effort is required from anyone to keep the meeting productive. Throughout, there seems to be someone ready to continue and lead the event in a free and unrestricted way.

You will find that in this type of meeting, someone will act as the organizer and will assume a degree of responsibility for the event. The atmosphere tends to be comfortable with little tension and the participants are usually relaxed. There is a feeling of support without anyone setting traps or trying to score negative points. The basic objective is one of having a relaxed, comfortable and enjoyable time.

2 Dinner party

The dinner party tends to be a more formal setting with a host and/or hostess. Dinner parties can be held in a very friendly atmosphere with similar objectives to type (1) above. The major difference from the friendly meeting is the presence of a structure. There will be some well defined stages of which others will be aware.

Formal dinner parties can be held to create a good impression or build and maintain a position of status. The host and hostess perform specific roles and will plan the event to the smallest detail. This allows the host to manipulate the people to achieve his objectives.

Discussion at the meeting will tend to be formal with one speaker at a time and the others giving polite attention. When there is a lull in the conversation, the host or hostess will feel the need to step in and maintain the process. The atmosphere could be reasonably friendly with the guests feeling slightly on their guard to watch that their behaviour matched what they felt was expected of them. Some hosts would have spent a great deal of time discovering facts about their guests to ensure that their needs would be met by whatever means was available at the meeting. In addition, the host and hostess will be in control and able to switch the direction of the event as they require. Therefore, the structure and discipline provide a setting for the achievement of objectives.

Difficult or outrageous behaviour is unlikely to be found at the dinner party meeting. The formal structure, coupled with the careful selection and screening of the guests would go a long way towards preventing any problems. Unexpected behaviour can sometimes occur. However, you will find that the actual setting and atmosphere work in strange ways on the behaviour of people to make them conform. This is, in fact, the power of the formal dinner party type of meeting. You could find yourself acting out a role quite different from the one you might want to perform. The pressure on you to behave in a certain manner would be there but its influence would be exerted in a subtle way.

3 Information

An information meeting has as its specific objective the passing or receiving of data. The meeting can range from the very formal, eg annual general meetings or speeches at dinner parties, to the informal setting of a club or pub. There will always be a specific purpose to the meeting where someone has a clear idea of what is expected.

The method of communicating the information can take many different forms, from human to electronic aids. The most common will be by a speaker or series of speakers providing information about their cause or subject. They will present their messages in different ways and hope to meet their objectives and the needs of the people listening. There is a great belief in the face to face approach as an effective means of communicating. However, in reality, it tends to be ineffective due to the poor level of ability of the communicators, coupled with inattentive listening. There is, therefore, a tendency towards complacency when it comes to the use of informational meetings to pass information.

The professionalism of communication through the media can contrast in unfavourable ways with the effectiveness of the communication by individuals at meetings. The skill and creativity displayed by those engaged in radio and TV is a fine example of how a message should be transmitted. If you can pick up some of their ideas of what to say and when, of the use of illustrations and visual aids to support the message, and involving the audience to clarify the ideas and reflect understanding, you will be well on the way to becoming an effective communicator.

Action point 45
Seeking/imparting information

1 List at least six ideas from the media on how you could improve your communication skills. Take each one and break it down into the skills involved and then relate these to the skills you have.
2 Describe how you could acquire the degree of skill you would need to improve your communications.

However, if you are part of the group being spoken to, you can still help the group achieve understanding. Previous chapters talked about the value of feedback; the same value applies in the group process where you can ask questions to clarify what is being said and provide the communicator with a better understanding of how the message is being received. Effective communicators look for feedback to check how they are performing. They need to know that the audience is in touch with the message and ideas projected and have a satisfactory level of understanding. This contrasts sharply with the less effective communicator who goes on and on, quite unaware of the level of interest and understanding of the audience. In either instance, you can help by being prepared to contribute your understanding of what is happening. In the latter case, it can be difficult to intervene; however, if your intervention is structured effectively, the desired result can be achieved.

The main benefit you can achieve from informational meetings is to obtain the information. To do this you need to be aware of the purpose of the meeting, the objectives of the people holding the meeting, the expected outcome and how you fit into the picture. Your level of understanding will be high if you apply your individual and group skills to extract the necessary information. When communications are good, you can help to make them better, and when they are less than good, you can help to make them more effective. One person in a group can make a significant contribution to make the end result meaningful to the people involved. There is a responsibility to check what is happening for your own satisfaction as well as for that of the others involved.

When you are involved in a positive way in the meeting your influence will be of real value in helping the group. The more you can focus on what is happening and reflect this to others as appropriate, the better equipped you will be to assist. This will place you in an excellent position when dealing with emotional events. The build-up of events when people become involved in principles involves a transition from facts to assumptions. This tends to make people feel threatened and they regress to an emotional level. At this point, all hope of a solution disappears until the situation can be returned to a factual basis.

There are many examples of informational meetings which involve emotion. You will have read in the press and seen on television many examples of how sides are drawn into a dispute or debate. The most factual and pleasant discussions can easily become emotional and conflict-charged events. By being aware of the ease by which a meeting can change, you are prepared to act in a decisive way to maintain it on a factual course. By keeping the focus of the event on the purpose, objective and expected outcome, you will be able to reduce the possibilities of emotional reactions. You will, however, discover that it is almost impossible to eliminate emotion, and at times it can be very useful to express emotion for positive purposes. What you can do is to minimize its negative effects and help the meeting fulfil its purpose.

4 Conflict based

There is no doubt about the purpose of this type of meeting as the antagonists and protagonists have their lines drawn from the beginning. The objective is usually concerned with coercing others to follow a particular line or course of action. In most cases the meetings are highly charged with aggression and emotion and with plenty of noise.

The principal people involved tend to be dominant and aggressive. They push, cajole, and threaten in order to achieve their objective irrespective of the feelings of those involved.

In many ways, it is like a scene in a theatre with the people involved acting out their prescribed roles. Once the act is over, they revert to being normal people again. This is often to be found in the industrial environment when union and management meet to negotiate. Observers are often surprised to see participants in an extremely heated and angry negotiation cease their hostilities and walk away to have a drink together as though nothing untoward had happened. The observers are unaware that the behaviour is expected by both parties and, were less expressive attitudes shown, the participants could be confused by the situation.

Most meetings involve some degree of conflict. The fact that we each want to achieve our objectives, even at the expense of others, sets the scene for possible conflict. The core of values and beliefs set in our minds over the years makes us vulnerable to challenge and when someone touches the nerve-end of a value or belief which we hold, we usually react in a hostile way. Our behaviour can be aggressive or defensive and in either case will involve emotion. This forms the basic recipe for conflict with neither party prepared to give way. The conflict creates an atmosphere which can engulf others who initially did not want to be involved but are eventually influenced. Once again, there is a role for someone to defuse the situation by attempting to return the meeting to its original purpose. However, this does present a tough challenge to the person attempting to intervene between the opposing factions.

Action point 46
Managing conflict

Describe what you understand by the idea of managing conflict. Can you think of ways by which this could be achieved? What skills would you need to achieve effective results?

A great deal has been written in management books about the management of conflict and these tend to suggest that managed conflict can result in positive outcomes. A skilful person can defuse an extremely hostile situation but usually with very few positive results being achieved at that time. What is usually achieved is an adjournment of the meeting for each side to review the position objectively. The subsequent meeting would then be held on a different basis, with less emphasis upon conflict and more upon achieving a conclusion satisfactory to both parties. The process involved is one of restructuring the meeting to a more formal basis with the purpose and objectives kept firmly in the forefront.

The last thing either side in a conflict-based meeting wants to deal with is the other party's facts. A mediator's role is one of clarifying what is being said by each party. When facts are agreed an attempt can be made to reach the common ground and then some move can be made towards resolving the issue, provided each party has the will and the desire to reach agreement.

A great deal can be learned here about human behaviour and about our capacity to ignore the other person's facts because they conflict with our own. If their facts do not support our view, they are there to be attacked and discredited. The process tends to be fraught with dangers and many casualties are found on the way. By using your skills, you can help to administer first aid, or even some surgery, to help the patient to recover. The meeting will then become productive rather than destructive.

5 Problem solving

The purpose and objectives of a problem solving meeting are usually clear but the means by which they will be achieved are unknown. The meeting brings together people who are expected to contribute to solving the problem. Suggestions are made and each one is considered until an apparent solution is found. At this point the meeting will usually end with someone agreeing to implement the decided course of action.

Many problem solving meetings fail to achieve their objective because of a belief that there is only one unique and easy solution to each problem. However, there is seldom only one right solution to a problem and the action needed to apply the solution is often difficult and complicated. There is a better chance of the problem being solved once these two facts are recognized.

Observing the differences between efficient and inefficient groups will show the best methods of approaching problem solving. The effective group will define the problem and identify its causes. The evidence will be examined in a systematic manner to separate fact from fiction. In most cases involving people, every effort is made to secure the facts from those concerned. Techniques for generating solutions, such as brainstorming, could be used in an attempt to find effective ways of solving the problems. The application of these possible solutions would then be considered. Part of the consideration would be to identify the adverse consequences of each solution. The group then decides upon the solution which most fully meets the objectives and implements this, monitoring the progress and fine-tuning the solution when required. The ineffective group would not apply anything like this depth of thinking and analysis to the problems encountered. Consequently the possibilities of success are limited unless they have a stroke of luck. The lack of success means that there is little satisfaction to be gained from this type of group.

A constructive and well thought out problem solving system has tremendous value for you in your life.

Action point 47
Seeking solutions

Draw from your experience, or from some other source, a problem solving system which you consider meets your present needs. List the stages and describe how they are applied. Think of a current problem and use the system to solve the problem. If you encounter difficulties identify the cause and develop ways of overcoming them.

It is important to develop your own problem solving and solution seeking skills; they will help you pass through any barriers which may impede your progress.

6 Contractual

A contractual meeting can be conducted within either a very formal and highly legal framework with little room for manoeuvre or a less formal atmosphere with scope for negotiation.

The rules covering the meeting are usually set out in clear terms and professional advice can be available to help the parties fully understand the terms of the contract.

The objective of the contractual meeting is to negotiate a contract. These meetings usually involve a limited number of people who have a direct interest in the objectives. Those involved are aware of their roles, the process and its expected outcome. The meetings are normally conducted by, or include, a professional specialist who leads the meeting on the basis of the facts and outlines the expected agreement. There are usually agreed rules to the process of the meeting which include adjournments to collect further facts or professional advice.

The most typical involvement in contract meetings is as a buyer or seller. Other examples are preparing a Will, exchanging houses, agreeing to get married or being divorced, starting a new job, or being transferred to a new position.

Action point 48
Contracts

> Spend ten minutes listing all the contractual meetings you have been involved in over the past year or could be involved in during the next.

We have indicated six types of meeting which you will encounter during your life. There will be many more, plus variations to those discussed. If you are expectant and aware of what is happening and can check this with the stated objectives, you are in a better position to play an effective role.

An objective in any meeting is one of being prepared to learn from the event. As you gain in confidence and are able to contribute more to meetings, you will develop a learning capacity which will pay handsome dividends in terms of personal growth. This will also be seen by others and you will become a useful resource in helping others to grow.

Expectations

The more you expect to gain from and contribute to a situation the more you will receive. If you attend and adopt a passive and uninterested role, the outcome can be predicted: you will be bored or ignored. Alternatively, if you attend and show an interest and keep up with events, you will gain much more.

Each situation provides us with an ideal opportunity to learn and apply new skills. They are the practice ground for your skill development and enable you to sharpen your effective skills and learn to use the newer ones in a better way. Developing a learning attitude to each event will increase your rate of learning. This will enable you to grow in strength and confidence as your inner self responds to the challenge. Your natural abilities will come to the surface and will provide you with the motivation to map out your development in a meaningful way.

The following chapters are concerned with translating your ambitions into reality and fulfilment.

8 PLOTTING YOUR FUTURE

There is a future

There is a future – today, tomorrow, next week, next month, next year, the next five, ten years and so on, but what that future contains is as yet unknown. It is uncharted territory through which you will steer the rest of your life. You can plot a course through that territory and decide how you want your life to be lived. You can influence how the future may be for you, your relationships and in the situations you may encounter. The future will provide many opportunities for you to develop and grow. Your future life plan will enable you to know which opportunities to pursue and which to ignore as distractions from your chosen course.

At the moment, you may feel either inspired or depressed about your future and that of the world in general. The predictions of gloom and despondency are often given precedence over those which forecast enjoyable and fulfilling decades. The more people believe in a stable satisfying future, the more they will be influenced to work towards seeing it realized. Self-fulfilling prophecy means that our future will take place in accordance with what we believe will happen.

Thoughts of economic depression, strikes, unemployment or wars tend to focus attention on those areas and can paralyse positive thoughts of reharnessing our talents, improving our total lives and achieving fulfilment. Since the future is unknown, you must prepare a plan of what you want out of life. The future does not have to be hidebound by the past, it can be free, and we can construct and reconstruct our lives in order that our true potential be realized. We have the brain power and resources to construct an effective future.

A fulfilling future may mean changes: in people, in lifestyle and in the world in general. A future planned on a sound foundation means that you will cope, survive and become enhanced and enriched by passing through these changes. Without direction, you may be thrown off balance by them and see the future only as a threat. If you know where you want to go, and believe there is a way through, you will view the future with anticipation and excitement.

The path to the future will have real and imaginary hurdles along the way. The hurdles are surmountable and it is a case of determining their reality and developing a plan to cope with them.

The choice is yours

Let us focus on you and your life in the future. To decide what you want to achieve in your future life you must consider some important questions.

Action point 49
Soul searching

Write down a short response to each question and then analyse the factors which relate to the answers you have given. How could these factors affect your future life?

Who do you want to be?
What do you want to achieve?
What will you do with your life?
What can you contribute to society?
Are you in control of your life?
Do you believe in yourself?
Have you other beliefs?
Do you want a better self-image?
Do you have faith in the future?
Do you have a mission in life?
Do you fear the unknown?
Do you live in the now or in the past?
Are you prepared to change?

In answering these questions you will arrive at achievable ambitions to which you can feel committed. In addition, why not stretch your thinking and expand your horizons to include ambitions which you had considered but discarded as being 'impossible dreams'. These ambitions may relate to developing something in your life at present or in areas unexplored to date. You may be surprised to discover that your dreams may not be as impossible after all. Therefore write down all your ambitions and dreams and whenever a new possibility occurs to you, add it to your list.

When you start to clarify your future ambitions into an order of priority you may find that there are a number which have a close relationship. These could probably all be achieved by using a range of similar skills and knowledge with which you can equip yourself.

Action point 50
What you really want

Refer back to Action point 1 and those in chapter 4 which deal with your future life. Answer the following questions based upon your improved awareness and skills.

What do you want to achieve in the future?

a) Describe what kind of person you want to be. Include a list of as many attributes as will be required.
b) List what you want to achieve in the next ten years.
c) Review your answers to ensure you have covered all aspects of life.

You now have an outline of what you want your future to be. Check to ensure that you have not allowed your choice to be restricted by negative thinking and that you have been prepared to include on the list ambitions which may require a change of attitude and which may take you into areas requiring new methods and ideas. The risk involved is probably only in your mind.

You need to develop a clearer picture of what you aim to achieve in the future. If you remain with a long list of dreams and ambitions you could be overwhelmed by the complexity of the task. It is helpful to focus on your future by looking at its aims in a systematic manner.

Action point 51
Order of importance

1 Review your list from Action point 50 and place the items in order of importance. Against each one state the reason why.

2 As suggested you may discover that several items on your list have some logical connection. These could be grouped together to form a major ambition with a number of sub-ambitions. The purpose of this part of the process is to arrive at a comprehensive and understandable list of ambitions or objectives.
3 Establish a timescale for each of the objectives. State the reason why you believe it would take that time.

When you have developed your list of objectives in their order of priority you will discover that the timescales could vary considerably. This does not matter so long as you can visualize the timescale for the total picture.

Defining your objectives

The sharper you can make your objectives the more likely you will be able to steer a course towards achieving them. The following process has been developed to help you prepare a clear statement of your future.

The first step is to write a short statement of the overall philosophy and purpose of your life. This statement should set out what you want to be, what you want to achieve and what you want to contribute to life together with the timescale and criteria for judging success.

The second step involves reviewing against the statement each of the objectives you have already developed. When an objective is not consistent with the rest you need to determine its significance and whether it needs to be rewritten or discarded.

The third step is to group together the revised objectives for each area of your life. Each group will include the main objectives which will lead to the achievement of your ambitions.

These stages are vital in the development of your plan. It is essential to take the time to make sure each stage is compatible and your statement and objectives are clearly defined, with a timescale and criterion for judging success.

The trail of unfulfilled ambitions can be traced to good intentions which evaporated due to lack of clear objectives and planning.

The following diagram illustrates the steps.

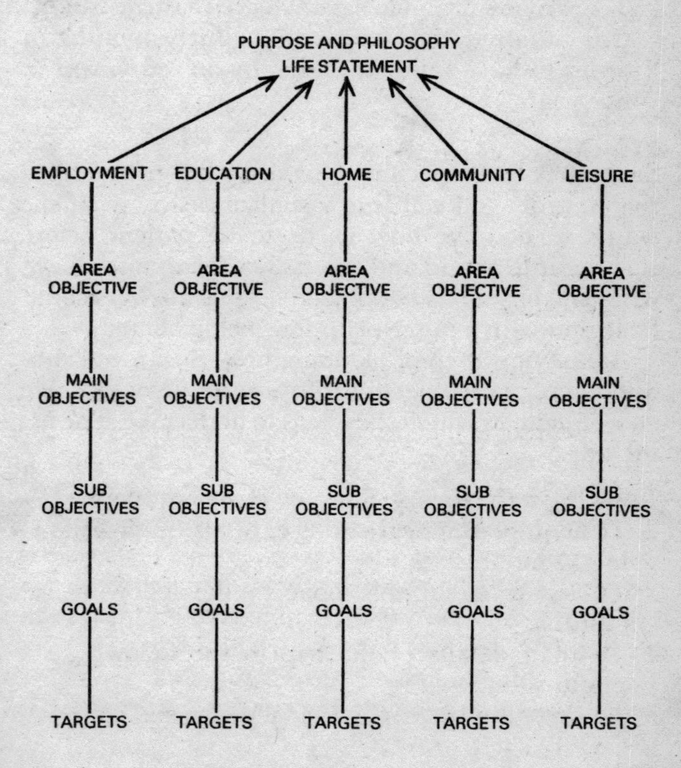

Future life profile

The following example will help you to understand the process.

Susan retires in five years time and as part of her overall purpose and philosophy for life she is very keen to increase her knowledge and capabilities in leisure activities to ensure that her future life continues to be active. To meet this she stated the following as one of her main leisure objectives.

> To learn to sail and to have achieved a single handed two hundred mile trip within thirty months in order to have sailing as a hobby on retirement in five years.

Susan has been specific in detailing this main objective in order to be able to visualize clearly what she wants to do. She now needs to be patient before rushing into action and assess 'how' she can achieve what she has set as her objective. The answers could be legion with a range of options being offered.

As the next step of planning how, Susan will subdivide the main objective into a series of measurable sub-objectives which she needs to undertake. The list includes:

1 To learn the theory of sailing in six months
2 To acquire practical sailing expertise in the following 12 months
3 To locate a suitable boat in the following six months
4 To plan details of the trip in the following six months
5 To carry out the trip in the following six months

This should help Susan focus on specific areas which she needs to achieve to meet her objective. Not only does she now know what needs to be done but she also has a picture of how each part relates to the other. The value of stating an expected time for each part can be realized when she moves to the next step of identifying the specific goals for each sub-objective.

Taking the sub objective 'to learn the theory of sailing in six months' she identified the specific goals which should be set to enable it to be achieved. These include:

(a) join a sailing club – first month
(b) attend training classes – following five months
(c) find club members with sailing experience and discuss ambition – continuous over six months
(d) read book on sailing theory and practice – continuous over six months.

She will apply the same process to each of the other sub-objectives to establish a detailed framework of goals for the main objective.

You may now consider that sufficient details are available to enable Susan to proceed on the journey towards achieving her objective. Susan now needs to translate the goals into action plans as part of her normal thinking process, visualizing each step required to achieve effective results with each goal. She will probably find some difficulty in remembering all the necessary action points and therefore she has proceeded through the following steps of detailed planning by selecting goal (a) and considering what targets could make up the stages for it to be realized, and then continuing the process with the other goals.

Goal
(a) join Sailing Club – first month

Targets
(i) identify requirements
(ii) contact at least two clubs – first week
(iii) visit clubs and discuss membership, club activities, training activities, opportunities to crew and skipper
(iv) decide which club will best suit requirements
(v) apply to join club
(vi) join club – fourth week

The first point of action is to identify requirements and to contact the club; this ends with the final step of joining a club and thus meets the original goal.

Developing an action plan

You should now turn to your list of main objectives and carry out the following action plan.

Action point 52
Developing a plan

1 Take each objective and list:

   a) sub-objectives
   b) goals
   c) targets

   Continue this process until you reach the first point of action for each.

2 Ensure that your action list is in the right sequence and that timescales are realistic for each objective, goal and target.

As you work through this process it is likely that you will find it necessary to review some timescales. Look at the relative timescales for each part of the objective, as it is important that they do not conflict. When you have completed the analysis for all your objectives assess the result, align the timescales and remove any overlaps which have occurred.

This process will help you sharpen and clarify your ambitions. However, it would help if you were to set out in some visual form an overall action plan. This then enables you to do the fine tuning and make final adjustments to the plan.

Action point 53
Charting your plan

1 Produce a chart by week/month/year and fill in the actions which need to be taken at each period for all objectives.
2 Make any necessary adjustments to ensure that the plan will be achieved.

This plan will show you the course you have plotted for your future life and map out a path of achievement.

Look again at your chart and relate it to your main objectives and statement of overall purpose and philosophy of life.

Action point 54
Commitment to achieve

1 Will this achieve what I want to be and where I want to go in the future?
2 Am I committed to achieving these plans?

The answer to both questions must be a firm yes if you are to achieve fulfilment of your ambitions. If it is an uncertain yes, revise your plans until you can answer yes to the two questions without a shadow of doubt.

What you need in order to achieve

You now need to consider the skills, knowledge and experience required to achieve your action plan. Many of these skills will already be a part of your tool kit. Alternatively you may have defined an objective in a previously unexplored area which requires new skills. Reference to your previously completed projects on current position, individual, relationship and situational skills will help you define what is required.

Action point 55
Skills/knowledge required

> Refer to your master action chart showing progressive action stages. List the skills, knowledge, experience required at each stage.

Once you have identified the skills, knowledge and experience required you can compare these with those you already possess. By studying the master action chart you will be able to determine the appropriate sequence in which the skills and knowledge will be required.

Returning to our example, for Susan the stages of her sub-objective to learn the theory of sailing in six months would include the following goals on skills and knowledge required:

1 understand the name and function of the main parts of a sailing craft
2 know how the craft is rigged to suit different wind conditions
3 know how to sail the craft to make the best use of the prevailing wind conditions
4 know how to navigate by use of charts and compass

5 know how to calculate wind speed and plot a course
6 know how to swim
7 know how to tie relevant knots

The above list would include as much detail as possible and would cover all the necessary areas. The next step would be for Susan to identify the standard of skill and knowledge she possesses at present. This then leaves her with a clear picture of what she needs to learn.

If for example Susan's knowledge of relevant sailing knots is lacking, she needs to break down this goal into the following sequence of targets:

(a) Acquire a book on knots with illustrations of how to tie them
(b) Identify the relevant knots required
(c) Acquire the appropriate rope
(d) Practice tying knots

Once again the degree of detail required is dependent upon Susan's needs.

Referring back to your targets, complete the following action point.

Action point 56
Consolidating your plan

1 Review your list of essential skills, knowledge and experience which you will need to acquire against your current level.
2 Take each and develop planned goals and targets of how and when you will acquire these.

It is important to show the time sequence for your acquisition for each area of skill, knowledge and experience. You will want to know when and how each part relates to the others and how it fits into the overall objective.

Susan intends to learn to sail within the first six months. Therefore she related her need to learn to tie knots to her objective and set the following timescales against each target:

(a) acquire a book on knots with illustrations of how to tie them (within two weeks)
(b) identify the relevant knots required (within two weeks)
(c) acquire the appropriate rope (within two weeks)
(d) practice tying knots (within eight weeks)

Susan would start the learning after guidance on what knots she needs to become proficient in tying and in what order. As soon as it is appropriate to start she would plan to achieve the necessary standard of proficiency by the eighth week. This analysis of skills and knowledge and time required to achieve a satisfactory standard is one of the simplest yet most vital planning tools.

Applying Susan's example to your own action plan, you will also need to determine the shape and nature of help which you may require to achieve each target. When you need to call upon others for help, the planning will enable you to arrange how and when you can secure such assistance.

Your total action plan is now virtually ready. However you need to measure your success as you progress through each stage of achievement. The penultimate planning stage is for you to establish a standard of proficiency for each sub-objective, goal and target leading to the achievement of your main objective. It is this standard which you will aim for as you progress towards fulfilling your ambition. Each standard set should be realistic and attainable in the proposed time frame.

For example, Susan's main objective was:

> to learn to sail, and have achieved single handed, a two hundred mile trip within 30 months in order to have sailing as a hobby in retirement in five years' time.

and she might then state her standard of proficiency for this as being:

> to have carried out the trip in line with the standards outlined by a professional sailing association.

You should now apply these steps to your total plans as follows:

Action point 57
Success criteria

1 Assess each sub-objective, goal and target to determine the proficiency required to meet the main objective. Note the standard against each part.
2 Review and relate these to each other to consider how realistic your planning is.

Integrating the plan for action

You should now have a clear idea and understanding of the different stages involved in achieving your main objectives.

There is one further step to take to enable you to see the total picture. This is the preparation of an integrated plan based upon your master life chart including acquisition of skills, knowledge and experience together with standards of proficiency required and time scales for all areas. The integrated plan should also indicate where you need to secure help from others and how and when you will acquire this.

Action point 58
Action

1 Produce an integrated plan on the above basis
2 Action the plan

The need for planning

The plan you have drawn up for your future includes what you want to be and achieve, and when. It has been built on an awareness of the necessary tools and help from others which will be required. The steps through which you have progressed to plan for your achievement will show you the most effective path to fulfilling your objectives. Detailed thought and planning of your future life will provide you with greater motivation and commitment to achieve it. You know that a sound plan will help you achieve your ambitions.

Your plan should show you can achieve ambitions in all parts of your life and defines the integrated programme stages within a time frame. The plan gives your life a framework through which you can operate on a daily, weekly, monthly, yearly basis. The plan enables decisions to be taken as relevant to the overall content of your life purpose. The detail and structure of the plan is organic, allowing you to grasp opportunities and learn from situations as they occur.

Planning will help to make your life and that of others effective and satisfying. Constructive use of energy during the planning stage will prevent you from wasting energy when actioning the plan. The ability to plan ahead successfully not only means that the probability of achieving what you set out to do is very high, but it also means that you have more time to enjoy your life and your attitude should be more dynamic and relaxed.

9 ACHIEVING YOUR FUTURE

Achieving your plan

Your future plans will be fulfilled if you are committed to achieving them. As you progress you will be aware of what is actually happening to yourself, to others and in situations and can take this into account.

This fine tuning and adjusting of your strategy will be continuous to ensure that you stay on course. Each experience will provide you with a learning opportunity and you may find as the plan progresses that circumstances allow you to acquire the required skills, knowledge and experience at a faster rate than you anticipated. If this happens revise your plans accordingly and review the impact of this on other parts of the plan. You may also find you are able to cope with sudden changes which would previously have adversely influenced your plan. You may discover a need to carry out pilot tests or experiments at some stages in order to assess the most effective strategy and this will help smooth your progress.

The effective foundation on which you have developed your plan will give you confidence to achieve its fulfilment.

Hurdles

You should expect to encounter hurdles obstructing or diverting you from achieving your ambitions and you need to identify and plan to overcome them as part of your overall strategy. Hurdles may be intrinsic or extrinsic relating to mental, physical, emotional, or spiritual areas. They may relate to yourself, your relationship with others or to particular situations. Hurdles may be real or imagined and your future success will depend upon your skill in identifying them.

Some may argue that by thinking about hurdles you are conditioning yourself for future failure; on the other hand, it could be argued that we often fail to achieve because we do not acknowledge that hurdles will be encountered. A positive mental attitude will help you not only to see the bright side of life but also see the negative issues and face them with positive solutions.

The most common hurdle people have to overcome is the negative power of their minds; its programming into a positive mode takes time and effort.

Contingency planning

As part of the process of overcoming potential hurdles, it is a useful technique to develop contingency plans. These do not normally alter your overall ambitions, but may guide you along alternative paths towards your objectives. These optional routes may take longer but will nevertheless lead forward. By developing contingency plans you will not feel trapped or despondent if your chosen path is suddenly blocked by hurdles. You will need to review the change to assess the effect that it will have on the rest of your plans and to ensure that all your objectives remain consistent with your overall life statement.

It's a dynamic process

There are two levels on which you can determine when you want to achieve your life goals. One is short term – today, tomorrow, and the next few months, and the other is long term. To achieve anything in life requires thought and commitment to develop short and long term plans to achieve your objective. With effective planning short term decisions become much easier because they are taken within the context of the longer term plan. This gives direction to your life and means that the long term plan has a greater possibility of success. As you progress through life your long term plans will need to be flexible enough to incorporate any changes you wish to make. How far you plan ahead is your decision as it will depend on how comfortable you feel about projecting your life into the future.

Once you have started the process, modifying and clarifying of objectives further into the future becomes easier. The development of a whole life plan enables you to achieve ambitions for all parts of your life and you can decide the importance of each part as you progress towards achieving your defined life purpose within a dynamic process.

Feedback

In achieving your plan, as discussed, you need to obtain relevant and constructive feedback. This will build your confidence and help you overcome difficulties. By recording your progress towards achieving your goals you will know why you have been successful and increase your confidence. You will also be able to update your plan in the light of feedback ensuring that when you do achieve success, the plan continues to be relevant and meaningful. It is for you to seek feedback actively from the opportunities provided by interaction with people and experience in situations. You will continuously learn about yourself and increase your level of awareness of honest feedback.

Feedback will let you know how well you are progressing and whether your strategy is working. Seek it and take action where necessary. Responding to legitimate feedback will help you to achieve your future on a sound basis. You can help people to give you feedback by explaining the purpose of your request.

Help from others

Help from others can be given to assist you to acquire skills, knowledge and experience. Others are needed to give you feedback to help you to plot your present position and chart your future with more accuracy.

Help from others will enable you to move consistently towards your ambitions and will enable you to keep on course. The interaction with others in a variety of situations provides a constant measure of performance which enables you to be aware of your progress and adapt and revise your plan as necessary.

Receiving help from others can also be used to provide them with help in their own learning process. Through your interactions you will be helping them to clarify, plan and progress towards their objectives. It may be that the best help you can provide is in having a consistent and positive attitude. By being clear about your own objectives you will help them realize that their lives may need a similar clear direction.

Advice and feedback will come from all quarters. Your family, friends, colleagues, boss, acquaintances and enemies will all add their comments. A positive mental attitude and determination to achieve your ambitions may expose you to some resistance from others. However a process of gradual change will enable others to adapt to you as you develop. They will then see how best they can help you achieve. You need to use all information received constructively for your future. As your level of awareness increases, you will be able to judge the help you receive and use only that which enables you to be more effective.

Counselling

You can obtain help from friends and colleagues. You can also receive advice through various counselling processes on a one to one or group basis. The main purpose of counselling is to enable you to come to your own conclusions through your own thought processes. The counsellor acts as a reflector or catalyst to help you work through the problems until you reach a solution. You will have a greater commitment to solving the problem if you have thought out the solution yourself than if someone else has provided you with the answer. There can be a very high level of learning if counselling is carried out effectively.

Counselling can relate to any part of life and can

be carried out by friends, colleagues or professionals. The principal need is for them to be trained in counselling skills. Three counselling processes on a one to one basis are now discussed and group counselling is dealt with in the following section.

First, there is counselling by a professional. These sessions cover a wide range of areas including marriage guidance and careers counselling. The primary purpose is for the individual to identify and clarify his needs, the cause of a problem or the potential for development in new areas. The counsellor will not normally be prepared to provide solutions. The counselling session should include a commitment from the person being counselled to aim to achieve the solution or action identified.

Secondly, there is co-counselling which is usually arranged through an informal network. Two people agree to get together and counsel each other on a specific topic. This could be a problem or opportunity at work, home, family, or leisure. The counselling sessions need not always take place between the same two people; this is the main value of a network of people, normally in the same line of business, through which you can call upon different people to help you with specific areas in which they have experience. The people in the network will be aware of what can be gained from the sessions for their own development. In many instances the exchange is a valuable building experience for the people involved. A series of sessions can provide considerable benefits to the individuals in the network.

Lastly there is exchange consultancy which is more often related to counselling on work topics. In this process each person takes it in turn to talk about their area of concern and the other person reflects and clarifies. Once the first person has decided on his course of action, the roles reverse and the second person is then counselled.

In any counselling sessions, the prime role of the counsellor is to listen. The counsellor must be attentive and interested in what the other person is saying and should demonstrate a willingness to listen and reflect. All forms of evaluation and judgement by the counsellor should be suspended, as the objective is to develop a climate which enables the other person to talk openly and honestly. By being present but saying little the counsellor will enable the other person to discover the factors which cause or affect their area of concern. Often the person being counselled cannot see the wood for the trees, and the problem has been going round and round in their heads for many weeks or months. By talking about it, the reality of the situation becomes clearer. Being prepared to be both counsellor and counselled during the process provides a better basis for helping others to help themselves.

The length of a counselling session varies according to the needs of the individual, but it is important to try to agree a timetable beforehand. Sometimes one session will resolve the problem area and other times a series of sessions will be required. At the end of each counselling session it is important for each to seek feedback from the other to ascertain the effectiveness of the session and identify which parts were helpful or unhelpful to the person being counselled.

Group counselling

Group counselling can be useful to break down your initial resistance to finding out about your level of interaction with others. Provided the feedback is positive and constructive, group counselling can play an important part in helping individuals gain confidence. Listening is the main aim for others in the group. They reflect and encourage that individual to answer the questions which he is posing about himself. Group counselling can have a catalytic effect on the individual. By making the individual think through various thought processes himself, there could be a lasting change in his attitude and in how he is going to achieve his goals.

Group process reviews are often undertaken at work, particularly after a meeting has taken place. The way in which decisions were arrived at and the contribution of each participant is analysed and reviewed with information being reflected between the participants. It is essential that this feedback be constructive with the purpose of improving the effectiveness of meetings and the individuals concerned. You can develop group counselling sessions where you regularly review and reflect each other's behaviour and attitudes. This will also help to strengthen relationships through improved understanding.

For both group and one to one counselling, it will be more effective if there is a clear understanding between the participants of the main objectives as this will enable issues to be clarified as they arise. This will increase the effectiveness of the counselling and help others to understand what is taking place. It is possible for the co-counselling and exchange consultancy to be carried out as a group session with an exchange of partners as required. There is usually on overall plenary session to reflect on the various roles which have been used during the session.

A mixture of groups and one to one counselling will be required at some time by most people to help them achieve their ambitions. To be able to talk uninhibitedly to another person will help you to clarify and focus on your real areas of concern.

Coaching

Coaching is another process by which individuals can gain help towards achieving their goals. Coaching involves identifying one or more people who have the knowledge, skills, or experience which you need to achieve an objective. As with counselling, the coaching process can develop over a period of time and vary in its intensity depending upon particular needs at any time. Coaching is often carried out at work although it is mainly associated with sporting activities.

A coach may coach one or several people at the same time. The coach will be giving the benefit of his experience through a process of analysis and solution-seeking. The coach's role is to help the person towards the required level of skill, knowledge and experience. There will probably be a planned progression to the level of skill desired over an identifiable period of time. The coach will advise and build on the current level until the required level has been reached.

Other resources

Positive use of the resources available to you will help you break down barriers, achieve the right attitudes, develop the right skills and knowledge which will eventually enable you to succeed. This does not involve just taking from others as you will also find others need your help to achieve their objectives.

Other resources are available for gaining the skills, knowledge, and experience needed, such as books, newspapers, professional associations, government and local authorities. You will need to identify the relevant source and how you are going to secure the help required.

By developing a network of connections, you will build on sources of help which will enable you to progress at a satisfactory rate.

Action point 59
Giving and receiving help

1 Review the areas in which you have identified you need help from others.
2 Review areas where you know others need help from you.
3 Review your plan accordingly.

10 LIFE IS WHAT YOU MAKE IT

Achievement

Every step you take towards your goals brings you nearer the fulfilment of your ambitions. The practice of determination and commitment will help you forward irrespective of the size of each step. You will not need to wait until every goal has been accomplished to sense the enjoyment and fulfilment of achievement. The very act of working towards the goal will provide you with a sense of achievement as you progress forward.

The act of determining objectives, translating these into goals and then planning to realize them will result in achievement. Life tends to be built around a structure which you then develop to meet your future expectations. The clearer you visualize the future and your place in it the more likely it is to happen. Although the future can throw up its share of difficulties and dangers, the reality around your ambitions will equip you to overcome the obstacles. As you face the problems and defeat them you will discover the satisfaction of achievement.

As you begin to realize more of your potential the fulfilment felt will motivate you to strive for further achievements. Progress in attempting the action points will provide you with a sense of achievement as they unfold an exciting future. The opportunity of taking full charge of your life can fill you with excitement. Once your plan has been made, and you embark upon the journey, every signpost which signals accomplishment will be a landmark in your progress. As in any journey the going can be rough and that's when your commitment comes in and finds a solution to the difficulties. Each problem solved and each goal achieved builds your inner confidence and strengthens you for the rest of the journey.

This in turn will contribute positively to other lives and to society in general. Your ability to cope with uncertainty and change in this rapidly changing world, and to exploit every opportunity, will have been vastly improved. You can enjoy the challenge that life brings and overcome problems in a way which will enhance your future achievements. This attitude will in turn reduce the stresses of daily life.

You and others

Your own fulfilment will also bring about a greater respect and understanding of others and the beliefs they hold. Although their chosen course may be very different from your own, they believe in it and expect it to satisfy and fulfil their needs and aspirations. Just as they cannot live your life you understand that you cannot live theirs.

You will feel comfortable in situations which are strange to you as you will be able to relate towards people whom you have not met before. You can listen to their opinions and attitudes without feeling the need to stress your own ideas. You will be able to put your ideas forward without the need to feel that you have to convert others to your way of thinking.

As you strive forward to achieve your objective the negative influencing factors in your life will disappear. They will be replaced by confidence, reassurance and positive attitudes. You will be your own person and your self confidence will grow as your self awareness increases and results in further achievement. Your level of achievement will become exceptional as your level of skill, knowledge and experience is integrated into your mission for life and fulfilment.

The realization that self development is not a selfish activity will be reinforced by the many opportunities you experience in helping others. The need of society to develop caring and responsible relationships is consistent with the need for everyone to accept responsibility for his own development. Life is a dynamic process which progresses forward irrespective of what we do. The more we contribute to our life, home, school, job and community the better society will become.

The important aspect of positive relationships should be seen by all as a means of creating a more caring society. You will be able to play your part irrespective of your age and place in the community. We all have something to contribute and our task is to find out what it is and then donate it willingly. The growth and achievement which can be realized from helping others offers a wonderful sense of fulfilment not easily obtained elsewhere.

Realizing the potential of your life

Fulfilment is the realizing of potential. It is the

release of that latent force which is present in each of us. You know you can achieve much more than you do at present. Unless you identify where you are going and develop the attitudes, beliefs, commitment and persistence to achieve more, your growth and development will be stunted. Life is full of joy and satisfaction but you have to work hard to achieve them. They are not given too easily. Part of the satisfaction is in developing and growing towards your goals and learning so much about people and life in the process.

The opportunity to 'realize your potential' is open to every one of us irrespective of age and position. For those who have achieved much out of life there is still more to be accomplished and probably they are striving for it. Those who have accepted less because they do not believe in themselves or have been stunted by others can now start on the journey. We cannot say that the passage will be easy as no one really knows what lies ahead in the future, but we can say that excitement and the joy of achievement can be yours if you apply the necessary energy to release your hidden potential.

In whichever aspect of life you find satisfaction this can be enlarged and new areas explored. Achievement comes from doing something better than you did before, or something new. Whether it is growing vegetables, climbing mountains or learning to swim, the sense of achievement is there. And as you fulfil your dreams and ambitions you will help others to realize theirs.